Dear Editor,   13th January 2010

    Congratulations on the 5 year anniversary of the
Stool Pigeon. I'm told you will be compiling a book
to celebrate. I hope to be included in that, though
I don't expect it will earn a dime. I'd be in it for
the infamy. It's a shame I only started writing for
you in the 6th issue but I've made up for that by
including some collage work I've done with scissors,
glue, and a copy of Italian Vogue.

    There have been 19 Son of Dave columns I think,
but i haven't been able to find them all. I've looked
all over the farm. The milkmaids use them to mop up
spills, you see. Could you choose one of the best and
include a snippet or two in the book? I'd be honored.
You never know when the lid is going to blow off
and Norwegian oil barons will buy up all the stock. I
want to be included. You can make little Son of Dave
action reporter figurines then.

    But until then, just more pages of print to
squint at. The ink runs into the milk and the cats get
lead poisoning. The saddle-hands have huge vocabularies.
It's old fashioned and quaint. Don't ever change, pal.

                    Son of Dave

WE NEED YOU LAZZARO, YOU LAZY, GREASY BASTARD

WE NEED YOU LAZZARO,
YOU LAZY, GREASY BASTARD

---★---

& The Other
Stool Pigeon
Columns

SON OF DAVE

JUNKO PARTNERS PUBLISHING

First published in 2010 by Junko Partners Publishing,
publishers of The Stool Pigeon music newspaper.
21a Maury Road, London, N16 7BP

thestoolpigeon.co.uk
sonofdave.com

ISBN: 978-0-9565246-0-7

Designed and typeset in Fournier by Mickey Gibbons
Printed and bound by Short Run Press, Exeter, Devon

CONTENTS

★

FOREWORD
By Phil Hebblethwaite,
Editor of The Stool Pigeon

These are tales of travel and adventure, freaks and visionaries, boozing and dope-smoking, fear and danger, and music. Always music. They sing something about the old days before advertising made liars of us all, and they poke the fire and fret, trying to stop nutting out about how long, difficult and fast this life can be. They politely demand you don't attack innocent people on the street who aren't part of the plot to sell you garbage and they take advice from a 92-year-old who has the answer to the oldest question around.

I first met Son of Dave in January 2006 when I interviewed him for issue five of *The Stool Pigeon*. I asked what a 39-year-old bluesman from Winnipeg, Canada was doing living in London and how long he'd been here (eight years by then). He said it was none of my business and refused to say. A few days later, *Stool Pigeon* art director Mickey Gibbons took photographs of him acting crazed and jumping off a chair in a room above The Griffin pub in Shoreditch. We ran the piece on page three with a quote as the headline: "I'm a one-man love arsenal!"

For the next issue, we offered him a column in our 'Comment & Analysis' section and told him not to mess its purpose; that the broadsheet structure of *The Stool Pigeon* was sacred and all columnists must, in a deranged manner or not, write pieces that comment upon and analyse music. I threw back his first two attempts and then, in some fury, he came up with 'Music magazines are agonisingly boring things to read'. It was exactly what I wanted to read in my music magazine, and I never gave him a brief again.

Son of Dave has been our longest-serving columnist and he's written some of the best stuff we've ever printed. He'd never been published before, but when that gate was opened he took us from England to

1

America, Cuba, China, Russia, South Africa, Australia, Canada, Egypt and back again. Sometimes he claims he doesn't have "any adventures to brag about" and I threaten him with an imaginary replacement. "A young writer, waiting for me to slip up and drop a stitch?" he'll respond. "Tell him to bugger off. I'll have something important to say by Tuesday." Once, near deadline, he was camping in Canada: "I'm just waking up here. Making tea on a Coleman stove by a waterfall in British Columbia. FUCK YOUR PAPER! I'll see what I can do."

Right before publication of this book, Son of Dave got in touch saying he was ashamed of the profanities in his stories and asked me to print the following: "Please forgive the swearing and remember that there are always a couple of savages down here at the front." As you'll gather from his 20 columns (the full collection to date), he likes the idea of a savage and I remember Mark Twain once writing: "We have not the reverent feeling for the rainbow that the savage has."

March 2010

2

MUSIC MAGAZINES ARE AGONISINGLY
BORING THINGS TO READ

Issue 6, April 2006

The only way I get around town is on public transportation. Cabs are expensive and I don't own a car because I like drinking too much. It's nice to see the city and all its freaks from the window of a bus. If I have to take the underground, to get to a soundcheck on time, for instance, I'll read a book. But never a music magazine. If you're reading this, you are an optimistic sonofabitch, but I think you're looking for knowledge in the wrong place, my friend. Let me tell you why.

The band interview: The worst place to look for good information. In the unlikely event that the musicians in the band might have something interesting to say about politics, or art, or automobile sabotage, it still won't make it to print because the journalist wants to write about music. On and on they will blather about music; how they came to make music; how they made music; how to make music; why some music is better or worse than other music... If people see you reading this vacant trash in the office, they'll think you're simple.

The album review: If you want to find out which records to buy to make life more bearable, you will never be able to choose by reading record reviews. It is the journalist's job to review records accurately, but it is their fear that they will get it wrong. Fear will always win. Therefore, they will never stick their neck out to say something is great until they've read it somewhere else five or six times. And they won't have the courage to say something is crap for fear that they missed the point. So they will take easy shots at weak albums and champion the safest middle-of-the-road poop until told to do otherwise.

The feature: This is a strange thing where the journalist reprints the band's press release and biography. It will say what the record company wants to appear in the magazine. Sometimes the journalist will add things or subtract things, but not often.

The live review: This is very interesting to the musicians who are being reviewed. Hopefully the live review will say what they wish to hear — that they rocked, or crooned, or sweated, or swooned. And possibly they did. There may actually be some truth in these reviews: they took to the stage, the sound was awesome, people loved it. But it's dull as the wrong end of a nail to read about.

The ads: They all say "OUT NOW" somewhere in the ad. I want to murder them.

The photography: A hefty amount of money, energy and hair gel is wasted on photo shoots for these magazines. Firstly, the band already has thousands of photographs of itself which could be used, but because the magazine prides itself on a job well done and wants exclusivity, they will spend up to £20,000 hiring a photographer, stylist fag, wardrobe bitch, make-up chick (who always gets laid), and catering to make the band look... exhausted. You can cut out a sexy photo of your favourite junky and put it in your briefcase while people on the bus point and laugh at you.

The classified ads: This is the only bit worth reading. Very funny.

And finally it must be said that the sheer number of bands being examined is staggering. How are you to sift through all that shit without feeling ashamed of yourself?

Many years ago, on the way to a photo shoot for *Rolling Stone* magazine (I believe this is irony, but I'm not sure), I was stuck in the back of a van with a band, in gridlock, somewhere in Midtown Manhattan. The heat was relentless, as was the noise of car horns and sirens. It was one of my first visits to that place. I was observing everything.

I could see little things happening all around us. On the right sidewalk, two old buggers had their sofa put right against a chain-link fence in the middle of this insanity and they were just sitting and chewing the fat.

On the opposite sidewalk, there was this rich urban bitch with her dog, looking in a window at something, paying no attention to the SIRENS, which were putting pressure on all of us from behind. Still gridlock. Almost no motion.

Our manager's assistant, who had been complaining of a hangover from the Russian samovar-flavoured vodka the night before, suddenly barfed into a plastic bag. She wasn't done and ran into a Chinese restaurant to continue. The van edged toward the curb to let fire engines pass. We had to wait for an old Chinaman to push his wheelie bag across the road. He parked it outside a corner store and went in.

The old guys were still talking above the noise and gazing at the fancy dog, which was taking a dump on the sidewalk opposite them. The owner began the ungodly process of picking up the turd with some newspaper, of course. We were late for our important photo shoot. Traffic moved a few feet forward. The sirens were deafening.

The woman with the dog and the turd in the paper looked around for a garbage can to put it into. Under the stress of the heat and noise and traffic, she mistook the Chinaman's wheelie bag for a garbage bin. In went the turd, and off she went.

The old sages on the sofa looked on as the Chinaman came out and discovered a stinking shit in his trolley. He screamed into the day. I inhaled deeply on a customised Camel cigarette and, as the manager's assistant climbed back in the van, we found an open lane of traffic to swing into.

I was high on the moment. This was living! I turned to the drummer and asked him if he saw any of what just happened. But he had been reading a MUSIC MAGAZINE and had missed it all.

We got our photo in *Rolling Stone* and there was a little paragraph underneath that said something from our press release. I cut out an ad in the back of the magazine offering an item which could turn a harmonica into a midi-synthesizer.

So you see, not only is it a waste of time to read music magazines, but they will seriously stifle your ability to observe the fascinating world around you. And indirectly, that Chinaman's outrage was caused by gridlock, which was caused by so many people going off to be in unnecessary magazine photo shoots in Manhattan so that optimistic sonsofbitches like you can read endless interviews with bands that don't bloody matter.

BECK HAS SCIENTOLOGY,
BUT I HAVE A BIGGER MOJO

Issue 7, June 2006

It's true: he's a fully-fledged, has-been-for-years, L. Ron Hubbard-loving weirdo. Look it up, it's not a rumour. Beck Hansen's father, David Campbell, is one. He's also an incredible arranger of strings and shows it on *Sea Change*. His mother, Bibbe Hansen, is one. So is his wife. And he replaced his band members with Scientologists. It really gets me steamed. What's so great about Scientology that it has to claim the brain of our number one funky kid?

Curious about Scientologists? They actually have some clever methods for learning to control one's happiness, emotions and successes. It's very expensive to keep up the sessions, however. As you move across *the Bridge* to the *Clear* state, there are further wisdoms and teachings which you have to pay for. The highest and most secretive level used to be taught to you on a yacht with Mad Ron himself throwing you overboard if you didn't follow the rules of happiness. He became very wealthy. But he's dead now.

The practices of Scientologists are popularly debated. They are secretive and have many celebrities on board who become elusive and irate when questioned about it. When new little Scientologists are born, they are left in their slime, wrapped tight and ignored in complete silence for the first couple days. That's part of breaking the bonds of family and encouraging commitment to the group. Maybe there's something to it, because many seem to become very successful people, and happy, in a suspicious kind of way.

Now, I don't know if we should be worried about our boy-genius Beck using this pop psychology, self-help and science fiction to help him make sense of the world. He seems to be doing just fine. Or maybe he's in the grips of a nasty cult, can't get out and needs help. But one thing I can't stand is when someone figures they have the inside knowledge and the one-up on everyone else. HEY, YOU BASTARD, SHARE THE GREAT NEWS! Make us part of the enlightened. We can't afford the seminars.

John Travolta, Tom Cruise, Katie Holmes, Chick Corea, Juliette Lewis, Jerry Seinfeld and on and on the list goes. Those most hilarious men writing *South Park* recently had a merciless go at Hollywood's Scientologist celebrities. It became so bad that Isaac Hayes has quit. He was the voice of Chef for years, but he drew the line at making fun of Scientology and quit the programme over it. What a shame. COME BACK ON THE SHOW AND SHARE THE GREAT NEWS, ISAAC!

No? Well, that's alright — I know that I have an even better secret path to *Clear*. It's all thanks to my MOJO. You can't see it here, of course, but I have it and I'd be happy to show it to you if you are very well behaved. Let me tell you how I found it.

I was a young bluesman, walking on Dauphine Street in the French Quarter in New Orleans, much too high to find my friends. I couldn't remember the name of the last street I passed, so I didn't know if I was going east or west. And every time I'd come to a new street, I couldn't remember what the last street was called. I needed to find my stage technicians who were drinking in a rock'n'roll bar called The Cave. I needed directions to them so I could ask them what they had given me that was making me so high.

It was a dark and windy night. The only other people around were a lanky dude with an afro and his matching girlfriend who came sliding around a corner.

"Hey there, can you tell me where a bar called The Cave is?"

"Of course I can! I know this town like the back of my hand, my man!"

"Yes he does!" said his foxy lady.

"They call me the King of New Orleans, and you can ask me anything. I'll get you what you need and set you straight."

"Yes he will!" she said, and gave me a little smile and a giggle.

"Um, where's The Cave?"

Ignoring me, this smooth dude held out a closed hand containing something. "As a matter of fact I am gonna give you something that will help you find your way and make you happy like nothing else can."

I didn't take it.

"Go on my friend, you can have this."

He opened his long fingers and in the palm of his hand was a brown ball a little smaller than a marble. It made me nervous.

"Go on my friend, this here is your MOJO. Take it!"

He shoved this ball into my hand and I knew that I had become part of some overwhelming process that I would regret. I did not trust these people, and I became painfully aware that I have a problem with trusting people on dark streets in American cities. So what did I do? I did the obvious thing. I SMELLED IT.

I mean, I had to smell it. It might have been a turd. Or fine Lebanese hashish. But it appeared to be a seed of some sort. It smelled of hubris. I looked up at them and the looks I got made me realise I was being very un-cool.

"Man, what are you doing? You don't SMELL THE MOJO."

"Don't smell it, no," she said and frowned.

"Aww, geez, I'm sorry, I didn't know what it was. Hey, this is very kind of you, but you said you know where this place is..."

"Listen man," he said to me, "I'm gonna tell you where The Cave is, but I want you to listen to me now. What I have given you is magic. It's the real thing and it's gonna make you sing!"

"Yes it will."

"And if you would be so kind as to give us a little something in return, I would be grateful, and then I can show you where your friends are in The Cave bar."

He had me. I gave him a couple bucks. He looked menacing. I gave him a couple more. He asked for a cigarette. Then he gave me easy directions. I tried not to run as I walked away. I found my friends but didn't show them my purchase. I was extremely nervous then. I had smelled the MOJO.

What was I thinking? That dude had given me the key to the highway! I'd received a bona fide talisman from the King of New Orleans. And for a very reasonable price. It really does bring good luck. Since then, I have had a series of experiences that prove to me it works. I have been given GREAT INSPIRATION AND WISDOM from these experiences that I would be happy to share with you. I WANT TO SHARE THIS GREAT NEWS. So come into the cloakroom with me for a second and I'll show you a secret. Come with me before I'm too old a bluesman to give you what you need. C'mon Beck, just you and me and my MOJO. Leave your weird friends outside.

WE NEED YOU LAZZARO, YOU LAZY, GREASY BASTARD

Issue 8, October 2006

You can't buy a decent undershirt these days, goddamnit. You can look in any gentleman's shop, online underwear distributor, or high street discount store, but you won't find a proper undershirt. Maybe what once was a classic has changed to the new 'muscle shirt' design. An undershirt used to have thinner straps and the material was ribbed. Something to be worn under a shirt, not to show people how big your muscles are, or aren't. In the interest of selling people a new idea, and then a great load of undershirts, they somehow convinced the people that the old one wasn't right.

Isn't that what happened to R&B? Of course not exactly, but partly. There are some cool new grooves and tunes and raps and rhymes, but what was wrong with the old ones? Leave it to the museums, we've got a load of new shiny shit to sell.

Lazzaro! Where are you, you greasy bastard, you? I'd rather wear one of your chilli-stained undershirts than this fuckin' thing I was sent by a man in Italy. He assured me he was sending me a real undershirt, like the kind the fat illegal Cuban immigrants wear in San Diego. I'm not going to stop trying until I find that lost moment when we had the perfect groove in a cockroach hotel in San Diego 15 years ago.

It seems whenever I'm too fried to be walking on the wrong side of town, I find myself there. I'm lost and unable to remember if the last street was a higher or lower number than the one I'm looking down. I may have mentioned this problem before. It's happened many times where they number the streets. And sometimes where they name them.

Who do I ask for directions? It's starting to look like a Mexican army barracks around here. Tired and hungry now. So hungry. Mouth so dry.

Where are my rock'n'roll technicians? They said... Oh, here's the piece of paper. The Flamingo on 108th Street and L Avenue.

I'm gonna ask that guy over there. He's fat and not too tough looking. Oh no, his friend looks like he's packin'. Shit, too late, they're staring. I wonder if they think I was casing them. Damned, I have to ask them.

"Hey guys, can you tell me which way towards L and 108th?"

"Hey man, that's a long way away. Chew gonna walk there?"

"Yeah, I got some friends..."

"Hey man, chew look tired. Are chew hungry? Why don't you come in for some rice and beans?"

I really don't think I should go in with these guys. But he's fat and probably makes good rice and beans. No way. They're gonna rob me and stab me.

"Hey, I'm Lazzaro, and this is Pete, and we're goin' in to my place here for some rice and beans, and chew welcome to join us."

What the hell. I'm gonna get robbed on the next corner anyway. Maybe I can have a meal first.

How do they package and sell you such a fuckin' ugly tie? Do you only wear it because you're supposed to for your job? Do you think it's nice? Are you hoping not to be recognised by the other men on the trading floor whom you fucked over for hundreds of thousands of dollars yesterday? I guess dressing up in wallpaper works like that. Why don't you just wear a hoodie and some Nikes for a quicker getaway to your Tinted Window Titmobile and off home to your boring wife?

The stabbing pain in my lungs must be from the cigarettes. I can't have a drink without one it seems. I can't have a drink without another drink. I can't get over the hangover without a good joint. May as well put some tobacco in it. Addictive. Like money and power and violence on television.

And speaking of which, how did 50 Cent get in charge of the pop charts last year? He's got a sweet voice. Good body. A way with the ladies. But what is it about saying, "I'm on the edge, I'm just waitin' for some nigga to push me, put my hand on my strap, what you lookin' at,

11

pussy?" that drives the kids wild? There's nothing new here exactly; there have always been tunes about how armed to the dick someone is and how he's gonna get the guy who touches his money or his women. I think the Irish wrote lots of them. But somehow music has a short shelf life, and catching up on the raunchy old reefer and ride songs of the forties isn't on the list of things to do for a sprouting young buck, and nevermind Irish revenge ballads two centuries old.

So off goes Billy to buy his hip hop, and whether he becomes a gangster, video game addict, or a stockmarket man, they sold another new shiny piece of shit. Send me to Nike Town if I ain't right. "Better watch what you say when you talk about me, 'cause I'll come and take your life away." Sell out, tough guy, and kill someone while you're at it, just to prove your songs are worth buying. Your undershirt was made in China, though. Not classy.

The stabbing pain in my neck makes me sure The Woman is sticking pins in dolls. Wouldn't put it past her. She's a vengeful witch, but had a way of turning a garbage bag full of unwanted clothes into a man trap. A little tear here, a little polyester there, and presto, yesterday's discards hanging off her like they're ready to drip off and leave her puffing and huffing in the summer night. Oh sorry, I'm desperately trying to remember the wrong moment and getting a little horny. Pointless.

Lazzaro, you unwashed illegal immigrant of a man, we need you! Why didn't you come to the show? You were on the guest list. I was gonna repay you.

In Lazzaro's apartment, there are cockroaches everywhere. Salsa is screaming out of a cheap radio and an ancient Spaniard is on the grimy sofa playing his stoned heart out hitting a Coke can with a fork. Perfect rhythm, strange smell.

I don't care. I'm so hungry and thirsty I will consume anything. I will take the plate he is handing me. I can't hear what he's saying but I'm finding a fork on the table. (I want two fork on the table, I want two sheet on the bed...) A cockroach runs back into the pot of beans. It is delicious. Better than any I've had elsewhere. I am handed a glass of water. They have no money for beer, it's obvious.

Lazzaro doesn't care. The old man also doesn't give a shit that a sickly white man has come into their place to eat food without any introduction. I wonder if we will say anything, or if the radio will be turned down enough so we can yell. I want to curl up and sleep on the floor by the broken television. There is an air vent there.

I wish I were there now. But in London there are sirens sounding out the next reason to arm myself to the teats. We're all gonna cough up blood and die after the suitcase goes bang. A cloud of smoke and debris and that's your last supper. Fuckin' crazy religious sickos on both sides. Can't we keep religion separate from armed idiots? Or religious idiots separate from explosives? Or idiots separate from religion? Or government separate from people?

Or am I just buying the new fear and war from the television because the last one wasn't good enough?

I'm getting an old friend in Canada to send me 12 dozen old man's undershirts he found in a warehouse. Previously worn. I'm going to get oxygen cylinders, barricade the door and seal the cracks. Keep the sickos out.

Lazzaro's kitchen is on fire but no one cares. We've found the perfect groove. The neighbours are irrelevant and our pounding jam is tremendous. The little radio has vibrated off the counter and is blaring trumpets and Cuban women. The old man on the sofa is disappearing in the haze. The television is two congas. The lamp shade a cowbell. The walls the bass. Another joint is required.

But why haven't you come to the show, Lazzaro? I put your name on the guest list. Were you too poor to get there? I think you were just too lazy, Lazzaro. Yes, too fat and lazy. I envy you, hombre. I admire you and I envy you. Your undershirt was perfect and your music timeless.

GONNA LAY DOWN MY HEAVY LOAD
DOWN BY THE RIVERSIDE

Issue 9, December 2006

"The brilliance, the versatility of madness is akin to the resourcefulness of water seeping through, over and around a dike. It requires the united front of many people to work against it." F. Scott Fitzgerald

It was a summer of mental health awareness, screaming saxophones and Bulgarian wedding music that lured in the crazies on the South Bank of the Thames. It wasn't approved by the Arts Council. It was spontaneous every time and only slightly illegal. We drank and danced on the riverbank on hot summer nights to spite the city, the terror and the lunatics in charge.

The problem with London is you can't go for a walk at night anywhere. The parks are shut, the heath too murderous. The high street is coughing up smoke, noise and sloppy drunks (God, I hate sloppy drunks) and you have to go pretty far into the suburbs to find a pleasant neighbourhood with trees on the street. No, Notting Hill Gate is not a pleasant neighbourhood with trees on the street! It's highly alarmed and patrolled by money-grabbing assassins.

On one of the last lovely days in August, the Barfly in Camden and Southern Comfort paid a lot of money to us for some blues exorcism. Free hooch and cash in hand. Only a few hangers-on from the afternoon gig; a couple lesbians, my record producer and right-hand man Alex, and some Germans. All day we tried to find a good argument in Camden Town but there was none. The evening grew dark but it was too beautiful to go inside and pay to see a guitar band or breathe the foul carpet in a crowded pub. For the last time this summer, we went to the South Bank.

A few benches along from the London Eyesore, you could find us on perfect warm evenings playing 60-year-old records on new battery-operated picnic turntables, or just listening to the Piano Lady (bless her fine thin frame). We drank champagne, wines or vodka. Fresh faces would pass through all night sharing beer or cheap cider. There were strong smokes and conversations over the moonlit river. It went on until the sun came up every time. All the gherkins and Russian sausages you could eat and whatever was leftover was gathered up by the homeless and the crazy.

'Let's Go Out Tonight' — John Lee Hooker
'Down By The Riverside' — Sister Rosetta Tharpe
'Wolf Call' — Earl Washington

"My wife and my doctor say I'm crazy."

"You probably are," I tell him. "Sit down, you're making me nervous. You want some sausage?"

"No."

"Well, give me a cigarette. You like ladies singing the blues?"

"It won't help."

"Well, try to forget the bastards."

'Baby Won't You Please Come Home' — Big Maybelle

The mad would arrive in the very early hours; those ones who admitted being mad. The homeless would just put down cardboard and go to sleep earlier, around two or three o'clock. We wouldn't even notice them. They felt safe sleeping by the music and bottles.

There was always a sexy woman. My record producer would make sure there was a sexy woman to dance with (and vodka, and cigarettes), and I would dance with her. And so would the old men who sat on other benches for an hour before inevitably joining us and accepting some wine. They were my favourites. They had painful hearts and aching backs, but they could focus and they showed the girls how to dance properly. Better than I can.

But the sexy woman always found a ride home just as the sun came up, and I suppose it figures that she wouldn't call again or say, "Thank you for the night, guys," but just go away back to some boyfriend with the right sunglasses and iPod in his leather jacket. I always felt sad when

15

she left. I had been too busy changing the record and talking to the old men to really get to know her.

There is no place in London to walk at night where it is safe and pleasant. But what makes me snarl is that no one notices it's a problem. We are locked in after dark, or conditioned to fly to the lights and noise like insects. The homeless are all alone outside. After the theatre lets out, the South Bank is abandoned apart from nutters, rough sleepers and foreigners who don't know any better. The Spaniards... gotta hand it to the Spaniards. They pass by in small groups and always stop to dance. They quickly drain the bottles, though, and we must prevent that. They have cigarettes but it's difficult to make them share. And they leave after only four or five dances. They have somewhere better to go that's open until six the next evening, and being outside in the warm air isn't special for them.

'At The Party' — Hector Rivera
'Brooklyn Mambo' — Elmo Garcia Orchestra
'La Cumbia De Ica' — Sonora Lucho Macedo
'Canta Romero' — Soleares de Triana (trad. flamenco)

Sometimes if the party was dwindling to just me, Alex and the sexy woman, some young lads in hoodies would stop to talk tough and take things. It required patience to make another joint to buy them off and play John Lee Hooker again so they wouldn't punch me. Once they got quite lairy. The Bill won't patrol the riverside because they are scared, so some imitation officers have to be hired by the London Eye. They know this party and often stop and share smokes and talk about the daily crimes on the South Bank. I sent them the code, they came, and the lads quickly fucked off.

The mental health of a population is directly related to its architecture. The more they are contained, the more crazy they become. People hide things behind doors and in their stone-faced dangerous heads. The only hope is to pump them full of drugs and loud music and let them into a field a couple times a year so they get a false sense of being free. That is what most music festivals do to for the young and unimaginative. But if you try to find a small plot of concrete in your town where the cars aren't allowed, open a beer, play hillbilly music and dance with an old man, people look at you as if you are criminally insane. They will try to take your shit away or arrest you. But if you go into the right building and pay the price, you can bugger that old man, blare Wagner as loud as you can stand it, and the authorities will not bat an eye.

When the moon passes behind the Houses of Parliament and the music returns from sixties bump to the more nostalgic piano of Fats Waller in the thirties, people get terribly happy. Kissing and pissing into the river, hilarity as someone ignites a mouthful of sprayed hooch like a drunken busker and some coins are thrown into his dropped trousers. Most people begin to say goodbye and try one more time to dance with the one who's been dodging them. And then I'm alone with the residents.

"You think I'm crazy?" the stranger asked.

"I think you might be. Do you change your mind about things a lot?"

"No. Well, sometimes. So what if I do?"

"Try to sleep. Maybe opera will help."

'Aria (Bachianas Brasileiras No. 5)' — Victoria de los Angeles

The Piano Lady was not there on this last night. Maybe she was ill. She is so frail and fair, like a ghost from 1910. The Southern Comfort wasn't classy enough to offer her anyway. And the lesbians... oh no! What have I done? Breakdancing with lesbians? Am I bleeding? Yes, I am bleeding a bit! It's not too noticeable, though. Shouldn't do that on concrete. I must sleep soon.

"He had a sense of guilt as in one of those nightmares where we are accused of a crime which we recognize as something undeniably experienced, but which upon waking we realize we have not committed. His eyes wavered from hers." F. Scott Fitzgerald

I wrap myself up in my second-hand suit, hold my records close and curl up on the bench in the earliest rays of sunshine. I ache already. In a few hours, when I wake up in this circle of bottles, sausage wrappers and party streamers, it will hurt much more. I will have no trophy for the marathon summer but a scab. But I'm too tired to go home. Am I crazy? I am not. I have nothing to hide.

BELLY DANCING IS BEST OBSERVED
IN A LOW, RECLINING POSITION

Issue 10, February 2007

"Don't fuck with Aulad Ali," they say. Those are the "Sons of Ali", Arabs with the killers' eyes from northern Egypt, toward Libya. They aren't trading camels and incense anymore. "They will kill you like a chicken." I assure them I wouldn't mess with anyone other than the smallest criminals, although they are often the most dangerous. I'm being given lessons in Arab history and public relations by a mixed bunch of stoned Middle East people in a black shiny car darting around London.

Several years ago, I was in good company with the Bedouin, under the stars in the mountains of Sinai not far from Dahab on the Red Sea. For a small fee I had been taken by camel to freeze to death in the night with only a couple of old smoking desert men and some candles protected from the wind in sand-filled plastic water bottles. I crawled under a gritty carpet that had been left at this camping spot in the rocks where the wind was lightest. I slept and dreamed of coral reefs.

It's not too far to go to get away from loud music and drunks. Nowhere is too far to get away from the pointless ranting of club promoters and barflies when you have to get away. The only music I heard for many days was while sharing a good pipe with the local sons of tribesmen by the seaside in Dahab with the radio playing. The music that mixes best with wind and sand and frankincense is Khaleegy, or Gulf music — love songs from Saudi Arabia. Or else they play Bob Marley. Not music to drink and throw up on the beach to. The Bedouin hardly ever drink. They prefer to smoke dope, and some old men will have a little opium everyday to keep their peckers up (mixed with the right wild herbs and small animals, it seems to work for them well into their eighties). But a Bedouin with booze on his breath gets a tick by his name. Booze will dehydrate you and just doesn't seem right in those parts. Belly dancing is best observed from a reclining position on the ground. Drunks wouldn't be able to control the urge to jump up and make fools of themselves.

Someone's child had an inflatable plastic globe there on the beach. We filled it with smoke and laughed and batted it up into the stars. The young Egyptian, Israeli and English tourists were a few miles down the shore, being messy and horny in the discos not yet bombed by the fanatics.

Rashid El Majed, modern music from Saudi, through a small boombox and a Shisha. Fill the pipe with honey-tobacco and grass. Mind your manners and don't be afraid.

If I had stepped out of the candlelight in the desert and yelled down my phone in English, I would have got some cold looks from my hosts. Deep in someone else's land they don't trust us bloody foreigners, with good reason, as we pose a long-term threat to everything they love and live by. Here in London things are reversed, and my camel riding friends can't go to a hip hop club and yell on the phone in Arabic without attracting the bouncer. That's what's happening now as I'm hurried toward the door.

But I'm happy to leave, because I've got the fear again! When the American hip hop gets going loud, heads start nodding and the women get loose and everything's cool until the gangsta tunes start. Then the boys start walking with attitude and the hoods stand in tough poses by the door. If you're not careful, the fear might set in. Bad boys thrive on it. It spoils the night for most. How am I supposed to make this lady laugh with so much gunplay being yelled about?

The bouncer has followed me and my terrorist-looking friends right out of the club. On the street, it isn't a jeep and some fully linen-wrapped Bedouin that picks us up, but a couple flash Egyptians in a new Mercedes full of smoke and gaudy air-freshener. We're going to find a place for pipes and the dance of seven veils somewhere on Edgware Road. As the car flies north, they all argue in different languages and ignore me in the backseat. They tell me I'm hearing love songs from Yemen.

Jalese El Sh air, music from Yemen. I 'm not convinced they are love songs. Put on seat belt, open window, don't be afraid.

A year after the bombs went off in London, bombs went off in Sharm El Sheikh, and then Dahab. The Egyptian government suspected the Sinai Bedouin. The mistake there is that the Sinai Bedouin don't fight over politics and don't want to kill young rich Israeli and Egyptian tourists. They will, however, have long gun battles with police who try to raid a poppy farm. Thankfully, though, they don't sing about that and expect people to dance.

Edgware is alive tonight with neon and money. You could read about bombs and Middle Eastern politics in one of 50 heavily biased newspapers and sit and have a coffee and sweets. But if you want to find belly dancers and the backroom, you have to knock the right code, brother. They will let you in only if you have a genuine tent-carrying Arab with you who can vouch for your sobriety and character. We go in to such a sweet smelling and sounding place I won't ever want to leave.

Faris, an 18-year-old Saudi singer songwriter. Very moving, he plays some instrument I forget the name of, and has proven that the traditional music is the best. This is the desert sound, if ever there was one. They say he's a genius. They tell me it's love songs again, and I believe them. A sweet rhythm. I am not afraid. And belly dancing is best observed from low down in a reclining position.

I'm very satisfied. But restless men with cars want to go. We get into the Mercedes and off to a mini-cab office in south London where the driver wants to buy some Ghat. Again, fasten seat belt, get plenty of fresh air, and try not to spit the leaves out in the car. Fear may be unavoidable soon. The evening seems to be getting desperate, and the conversation more serious.

My friends tell me that in Dahab, three people blew themselves up killing Israeli and Egyptian tourists, a German kid and local Bedouin. Two of the bombers were from north Sinai and the other was a Palestinian. They were organised and armed by Palestinians, who don't generally like the Bedouin people and obviously don't like Israelis or Egyptian tourists having a dive and a nice meal. I haven't heard any good Palestinian music yet, so I'm not warming to them despite their underdog status.

And despite their status as Spoilt Rich Evil Zionist Empire, Israel has produced some great bands recently.

Izabo, from Tel Aviv. It's incredibly fun and poppy, but with some Eastern melodies and sixties' guitar sounds. The singer is hairy and cherubic. No fear possible. Drink Coca-Cola.

I am charmed by the Israeli pop as we speed up and head back through the West End. But now, to my horror, I notice the car is stopping by a stripper club beside Euston station, and the arguing is becoming louder. The Egyptians and the Israeli want to go in but the Bedouin and the white guy don't. I'm tired and I can't breathe because of the constant smoking and suddenly the horrid plastic air freshener has got to go out the window. Well, I may as well have crapped my pants with how fast I was thrown out of the car after the air freshener. I spent the rest of the evening talking to a life-size waxwork of Charles Saatchi in the Edgware Road subway. Don't believe me? Go there and look. There's too much freedom here. Makes us crazy.

A few years ago I was calm, warm, and enjoying some fava beans and eggs as the morning wind blew in off the Red Sea. My responsibilities were far away, and my money was worth a lot of breakfast. It would be another week until I flew back to London with a cheap rug and a few tape cassettes I scored for two pounds and some beat up brogues (I have no idea what that sand-surfing Mustapha wanted with my old shoes). I could almost smell Saudi Arabia from across the water and I'm sure they could smell my feet. I'm told it's forbidden for a woman to dance for a man over there. I wonder just how much the people miss that. I wonder if the suicide rate is high. Worse in London, I think.

LADIES, PLAY FAIR AND DON'T SELL OUT
YOUR SISTER ROSETTA

Issue 11, May 2007

The gossip in an old ladies' hair salon is nuthin' compared to the filth I'm hearing backstage while the new burlesque girls spend literally hours doing their make-up. It's all I can do to keep from suddenly exposing myself with a big clown's nose on my offender. I keep the thought to myself. Competition between these ladies is fierce, and the promoters will kill for a good venue or write-up in *The Times*. Oh well, old friends become new enemies, but at least the public is entertained after so many years of eventless nightclubs and guitar bands. At last we get high-wire acts, sexy contortionists and strippers with a sense of beauty and humour who don't rub their cracks on a brass pole. Well, maybe that's their other gig but it's not even an issue these days, is it?

Ah, the beehive and the beauty mole, the garters and terrible tattoos poking out from under pretty patterned skirts. We live in excellent times once more.

But the hounds are at our heels, my friends, and I envision every East End market selling nipple tassels and corsets instead of g-strings (revolting things) and studded belts. Right now, while we sleep, the major record label men are actively hunting 23-year-old lovelies who claim Billie Holiday as a major influence. They're offering £100,000 advances in the hope that they find the next Amy Winehouse. I don't know how they sort through so much talent. Hard-working fellows, keep up the good work! Ambitious and spread out on MySpace in Suicide Girl poses for all to see, it's a fishnet frenzy. I must buy a computer.

"It's a mean old man's world," sang Dinah Washington. Not any more it's not. The fairer sex dominate the R&B charts, Brit Awards,

AAA American radio, and even rock radio. James Blunt really isn't helping matters. But the danger is they'll desecrate the tome of early American music by serving up whorey, vulgar, watered-down versions of the proud and luscious original. I should know: I do it for a living.

The old style is everywhere: fifties girls on a Fratellis poster, zoot suits in all three types of MTV videos, and Marilyn Manson's ex-lady all over the popular press with her burlesque beauty lessons. The masses are finally being given a taste of what was covered up in the fifties by the rock'n'roll marketing machine and *Reader's Digest*. But the taste is a bit chemical, like a Smirnoff alcho-pop. You still won't get the real Martini. The shrunken, desperate record industry is looking to rape the young again. Shouldn't the good music and seduction be reserved for us grown-ups? The Ministry of Burlesque. A name that says it all.

Oh, how shitty it feels to be fleeced. In 2001, I was on my way to South Africa to do some shows. I was to tour with a band called The Flash Monkey, who were booked on the same plane. I radioed ahead to the promoter (a powerful lady I'd once had the pleasure of seeing swim naked with penguins) and asked what this band looked like. It would be a long flight and we could have a chat. "Oh, you'll see them," she said.

They were there in the lounge, an impossible group of antique gangsters with saxophones, hat boxes, leopard skin shoes, wide silk ties and even a big man from an old Las Vegas showgirl saloon. We got on naturally. We played to scant audiences of nervous white people in small towns around Johannesburg, screaming the blues, late swing, striptease and early R&B.

The promoter was, alas, not in love with me. My safari suit and camel hair tie were plain in comparison to these garish thugs. And I'd forgotten my hat. The sun beat down and burnt my scalp. I was out-done.

I still have scars from that tour. The lion safari left me unmarked, thank bald-headed Christ, but quad biking was a foolish idea. And a drunken golf cart race around Johannesburg Zoo got the authorities on our trail. I asked Jake if he was alright: "O' course I'm not aw right, I got a fu'ing golf cart on top o' me. Ge' it off!"

It hurts to be squeezed for your cash. Some get paid a lot for their good looks and a song. Others are doomed to work the streets and do things the hard way. I like the streets and I don't trust people who don't walk. The domestic workers smiled at me on the footbridge towards New Town. Then they looked curiously as I walked north into the centre. But by a South African mid-afternoon, as I was being held up by my neck like a chicken, strong men emptying my pockets in a crowded market, no one looked at all. No one cared. In my ear the bastards whispered, "I'll kill you, I'll kill you," and they do usually stick you with a knife if you struggle. I'd stopped struggling because my windpipe was pinched shut. This is why white people won't walk anywhere in Jo'Burg. I've survived a few ghettos, but they're still very traditional there. That's the last time I wear a t-shirt to fit in with the locals. Look good if you're gonna die at market.

I felt comparatively safe in the company of The Flash Monkey after that. Hard being such a fuckin' loner. We kept in touch in London.

In 2003, they started up the Lady Luck club in the basement of a tacky strip joint. The contrast from upstairs to downstairs was beautiful. Money and business suits went up, the poor went to the cellar looking like new tattooed nobility. Soon after that The Flash Monkey Cabaret began and nowadays sells out the Café de Paris. The 'new burlesque' and hidden music of the early 20th century has reached the popular media, but like a choked chicken or a thin white bluesman, it's about to be squeezed by sinister and traditional means. The same people that replaced 'race music' with Buddy Holly and Elvis are going to give you a little cleavage and saxophone over a drum loop. Think what Moby did with blues and gospel.

They told me that the woman in Rachel's Revels with the paparazzi was Ginger Spice. The gate's been left open and they're coming in to shit in our yard.

But we have live entertainment and old music back on the menu at least. A bluesman has a steady gig even if you, the public, are too tight to buy albums anymore. Ya might pay 70p for a download, but not if you can help it. And I'll bet you're gonna pay plenty for some old-fashioned looking Agent Provocateur knickers for the secretary.

I'm just drinking in the corner waitin' for my turn. Oh my hat, how does she fit into that? Does it have laces or hooks? A dressing room for champions, this is. Ladies, you're in full control, aren't you? No one's making you bend over like that. I hope you play fair and don't sell out your Sister Rosetta. Please let the past keep its glory. And innocence is not such a bad thing, ya know.

IMITATION IS THE SINCEREST
FORM OF TWATTERY

Issue 12, Summer 2007

Just a couple weeks back I was sharing a dressing room with an old sage, and he opened my eyes a bit. Honeyboy Edwards is 92-years-old and probably the last Delta bluesman left standing. He's a man of few words with a remarkable memory and history.

Clean, young couples and blues geeks come into the room to have their picture taken with the old man. A truly stunning Dutch beauty and her fresh-faced guy have just left. I say to Honeyboy, "That was one of the most attractive women I've seen in quite a while."

"She got a real nice ass on her," he replies.

Mr Edwards is sharing with me a sublime bottle of homemade spirits, which a local has graciously given him. I ask Honeyboy to give me some advice about women. At his age, he still gets more love in his life than this sorry ass grump.

"Sonny Boy Williams and I used to get a lot o' women when we was travellin' round."

"Really. Wow. Did you guys have a technique?"

"Sure. We'd beg for it."

"Gee, I haven't tried that."

"You try it."

"I might."

Honeyboy's set is perfect. There are no fireworks at the end, not much parlay with the audience and no looping pedals, just simple delta blues guitar and a weathered old voice. The first 10 rows are spellbound. Toward the back, people chat and send texts. Life goes on.

But I ask you, what would happen if Honeyboy Edwards took up playing the bagpipes? And I'll tell you, the world would turn upside down, fish would crawl up on dry land, and millions of civilised people would run raving into the forests and starve to death. Old Southern American black bluesmen do not play bagpipes. So why oh why do some cultured educated white men and women take up Mongolian overtone singing, climb a mountain in Tibet and flog themselves? I don't know the answer to that.

The great white imitator knows no bounds. Twenty-five years ago in the Canadian prairies there was a benign reggae band called Roots Soljah or some such nonsense. Fronted by a good-natured white fellow with dreads down to his ass, they had one very good song, 'Island Records Sign Me Up'. But I don't think they had a hope in reggae hell of getting signed, although they were a good band.

They were imitating something. Imitation. Westernisation. Constipation. Chicks loved them, though. Must have been the weed.

It's a simple fact that nothing goes so well together as Jamaican music and sensimilla. Homemade hooch and blues. Or peyote and Hopi Indian drum chants.

I don't think you can find wiser advice about the wicked ways of women than from an old Delta bluesman, but years ago as a young mutt looking for guidance, I was drawn further out into those prairies to visit a hippy commune where I was told a Hopi Indian prophet would be visiting to lead a sacred peyote ceremony. Well, wouldn't you?

These communal great white imitators had been living the good life, sticking strictly to the customs of the Ojibwe Indians for 15 years, solar panels and wife swapping aside. Some real Indian brothers would be arriving the second day for the ceremony. But first these bunch of lunatics were gonna teach me how to pray in an Ojibwe sweat lodge.

That night was the first time I'd truly prayed. Outside the dome of birch branches, caribou hides and canvas it was a beautiful snowy winter evening. All day a fire had been kept and under the coals were rocks the size of heads that glowed red in the night. One by one, over five hours, these rocks were brought into the tent and put in a hole in the middle of 10 naked hippies, as well as yours truly, and as the heat intensified and the drumming and singing became more and more unbearable, I put my

27

face down on the earth to suck the only cool air there was. I prayed that something good would come from this insane sacrifice of my patience. The next day could only get better.

Al Jolson. Done up in blackface and singing 'Mammy'. Great bungee jumping Christ, what was he thinking? How can one white guy get it so wrong and another white guy like Keith Richards get it so right? Music crosses borders and cultures and isn't owned by one kind of people. But you either imitate or become. Keith Richards isn't an imitator. He does things how he likes them.

But like Robert Johnson playing the accordion, our genuine Hopi prophet gets off the plane from New Mexico and comes walking into camp as white as my left ass cheek.

By 2am, I was choking back a second helping of yummy powdered cactus while some of the most seasoned hippies were retching up their first. The drumming and prayer songs were authentic and intense. The fire chief (commune leader) was shaping the embers slowly over hours into a huge eagle that burned into my retinas. Outside, the temperature dropped to -25.

It was the second time I prayed. I prayed for the strength to get through the night without leaping over the cinders, breaking the water drum to little bits and chasing one of the wives out into the snow.

This ritual was very strict. The fire chief was not to be fucked with. There were ancient rules of conduct and a fellow couldn't fart without asking permission. The one thing that allowed me to endure was when the drum was passed to the only real Indian in the circle. A true plains Indian, like a quarter of the population in the prairies. When he sang, a natural peace descended which I'll never forget. I wouldn't ever attempt to imitate that. Fucking pathetic wife swapping great white hippie swindlers, I'm gonna eat as much of this cactus as I can and then hitchhike outta here as soon as the sun comes up and I've raided your kitchen. Some never made it out of there for years.

More profound and arrogant thoughts as I'm leaving this coffee shop in Holland (where one buys and smokes dope) to catch a train back to dirty London: Why do they have to play Bob Marley and wear sunglasses in there? Why aren't there any women in there? Why aren't there cartoons on the TV, cold cereal to munch and ropes to swing on instead of an atmosphere of fear? They're imitating something.

Please darlin', come on back to my kitchen. You're so beautiful it hurts me here... I need you to love me a little. I promise I'll make you laugh and moan. I've got Captain Crunch, a jug o' milk and a big easy chair we can drag out into the garden. I'll wash your feet in Champagne. C'mon lady, pleeeease? Honeyboy would be proud of me if I could just bring myself to do it.

EVEN A RING OF IRON IS WORN AWAY
BY CONSTANT USE

Issue 13, October 2007

The hangover: puffy eyes, an oily and swollen face, sores on the tongue. Thirsty, but sickened by water. A poor sense of smell making you unaware of how much you reek of beer, cigarettes and urine. Sleep started with complete blackout but ended too early in a broken nightmare like a skipping record.

To have a drink would ease the pain, but that's the first step towards repeating the crime. Vigorous exercise can do wonders but can weaken you and leave you prone to disease, fever, twisted ankles. Eating fruits then heavy, greasy food helps but does not clear the conscience. The bowels are unpredictable; liquid horror, or constipation. Stinging anus. Shame and degradation.

Music will help to calm and distract from the acid pain and embarrassment. Debussy, *La Mer*. Or some soft bluegrass ballads. But the hair of the musical dog won't work. The techno track which caused you to do the twitch in front of the African girls will sound damned offensive today. Wailing saxophone solos will be dated and corny. Rock'n'roll is loud and stupid.

The alcoholic: someone who often chooses to have a drink in this situation. Once that pattern is set, the hangover isn't as bad, or almost non-existent after the third day. But the body will become starved of proper sleep, the emotions will become jagged, and bruises will appear.

Some alcoholics can function for years like this, with only short periods of sobriety. Other alcoholics will binge and make enemies and lose all control each time they pass the third drink. They are the Jekyll and Hyde drinkers, always apologising and moving in and out of people's graces. Sexy and charming to those that don't know them, but often suicidal in private.

"All aboard... the night train!" There is a train from Moscow to St. Petersburg for the touring musician to lose his mind on. Arrive at the platform in the dark Russian evening, steam gushing all around you and walk the 20 coaches to your cabin. The porters, conductors and ticket takers all wear green, round Soviet-era hats giving your trip a military feel. The ancient heavy train has no restaurant or bar on board, but if you are with a good interpreter, a knock on your cabin door brings some rough sandwiches and sausage. If your promoter is skilled and quick with dollars, you will be amazed: a knock on the door brings a bottle of vodka and six glasses, not plastic cups! Bring your pocket music-stealing machine and some speakers. Dance and be merry. There will be no sleep and vodka everywhere you turn for as many days or years as you like.

Our good hosts and promoters, Dmitry and his partner Angela (a wild Ruski if ever there was one), know the country's history well. Many Russians know it well, as each decade is marked with waiting, suffering and work. They value the truth about their history as a reaction to so many lies being told to them for so long.

Dmitry put us in a cheap, extraordinary hotel outside St. Petersburg, directly opposite the old palace of Catherine the Great. In this weird hotel, buildings from different decades of communism are linked by dusty corridors, and staircases make the drunken morning trip to our rooms take no less than 15 minutes. There are a dozen staircases up and down, paintings and statues of grim military and civil servants. Stalin himself left a brighter patch of wallpaper where his picture had been removed from every room. The meetings, bribery and murder which went on in that hotel are better forgotten.

Out for a walk. It's best to carry a large flask of vodka and a sausage with you at all times. Don't try bringing a portable turntable and all your old swing records. They won't let you into the palace with those.

The immense gardens and walkways leading to Catherine's abandoned and lonely bathhouse were just frosted over and the grass crunched and we walked silently, smoking and drinking in the sunlight. Dmitry had spent his childhood here. His blue eyes matched the colour

31

of the empress's palace. My blues producer (Captain Future from the Future Shape of Sound, who had brought me there as part of a small tour called 'Brit Wave') carried an old Soviet flask and plenty of smokes. We learned history from Dmitry.

By now you will feel sadness. It's everywhere there — in the Russian eyes and blowing in off the ocean. You've got to keep a good sense of humour and a big sausage to beat it off.

Backstage at the gig in St. Petersburg was a young Russian rock drummer with no neck and catchers' mitt hands who was no taller than 5' 5" but who weighed 250 pounds. Solid gristle. He would free-pour vodka from above his head into his mouth and it would wash down his throat without him swallowing. His liver must have been the size of a ham to filter more than a big bottle of booze like that each day. One of those bottles would kill me instantly. But he will live a couple more years.

In my cranky opinion, children should be taught about alcoholics and people with depression and personality disorders at school so they can cope with what's at home. AA. In the UK, it's claimed that 1 in 13 people are addicted to drink. The BBC puts it at only 1 in 20. By my calculations, it's 4.6m who admit it, and 5m who don't, making it about 1 in 7.

Instead of these sums, eight-year-old children are taught more complex (and accurate) mathematics about groceries. Mother shrieks and threatens to kill herself and hides the gin behind the cereal boxes. No one intervenes until bruises show up on junior.

I had just been paid a fistful of American dollars behind the club by a stranger with a tinted-windowed Mercedes. Some of us were put into a shiny Land Rover thing and swung onto a freeway. We were instantly pulled over and we had to give the police $100 to avoid a whole night in jail filling out forms. For no offence whatever. This happens all the time to those who drive flash tit Land Rovers in Moscow. Tee hee.

Avoid that. Just walk out on the road, stick up your hand, and someone will pull over. Settle a small price and most drivers will gladly turn into a taxi if they have the time. Sensible, really. A nice conversation in a Lada, also with tinted windows, and AC/DC through a small speaker.

Nowadays in Moscow, the rich kids are very rich and they go clubbing and you can dance and be merry there in the latest fashion. It's as chic as you like. But if you like to drink outdoors, and experience something different, go for the day to the park where the Russian Exhibition buildings are. There you can have a pony ride or fall off the go-carts. Most of the park has been paved over and everywhere are huge imposing statues of Stalin and countless other bastards. Sputnik is there and, bizarrely, an empty passenger plane you can climb on at great personal risk. A huge, ornate but dilapidated fountain in the middle of the park is circled by people of all ages drinking and throwing their tins and bottles on the ground. Hundreds of people drinking beer all afternoon. Not a bar or waiter in sight.

All over the park are abandoned government buildings that once boasted the achievements of the Soviet Union. Teenagers play drunken ball-hockey on rollerblades. BBQs and terrible music pollute the air. It is sublime. Unendurable unless you are drunk. And I was drunk again after several days and nights of it.

By the fifth night, I felt the gentle hand of wisdom on my shoulder telling me not to try climbing out of the second story window. I turned to see an old man with sad eyes who just shook his head. One of my feet was out on the ledge. My plan to use the awning as a first floor and a drainpipe instead of stairs would have ended in broken legs. He disappeared like a ghost. I finally found the stairs and peed in the alley. My producer looked down on me from the hotel window and threw me down a pillow and blanket to use on a bench. I couldn't drink again for two months. I will never drink through four hangovers again and rarely through even one.

The music industry and booze industry are inseparable. The worst face of it is a mud-covered, violent lad in a field in England swaying to The Libertines under a giant Carling banner. More distasteful than a Moscow park at night.

Alcohol sponsorship is the largest funder of the musical arts in the

UK and US. That has to change for the sake of the music and the poor rock'n'roll children whose fathers are down at the pub remembering the time their face was in *NME*.

The young masses are hardly ever passionate about music unless they can swill cheap beer and throw their plastic cup in the air. Indeed, they are told to do so. Clean, sit-down venues are for old folks or the French.

Russia is obviously headed for disaster. The main sponsor is a vodka company and the Yankee dollar is currency. To your health! Chanel and Starbucks have blossomed in Moscow and the poverty and corruption is as bad as ever. Every hangover is harder than the last.

Our friend Dmitry made it out and makes lovely music and children in London. I haven't seen him out for a drink in quite a while. I still drink from my producer's Soviet flask sometimes, after work in his studio. We hesitate to visit Russia again.

BE SURE TO SEND A LINCOLN
FOR THE ANGEL OF DEATH

Issue 14, December 2007

I saw the vortex and steered the two-tonne steel automobile into a lugubrious cruise around the outer edge. The car is Kyle's problem now, but back in the mid-nineties for 500 bucks we bought a 1963 Lincoln Continental with suicide doors, the colour of a faded band-aid and covered with lovely dents and rust. There was no better way to get around Los Angeles. And it made a good second home when I couldn't face the Magic Hotel in Old Hollywood anymore. I loved that place.

I'd been expecting the vortex of death to suck me in for a few days, so I saw it coming near an exit ramp to Pasadena and just missed crashing into a fiery shit-storm by inches. I knew it was time to leave the city for good.

It was Aristotle who pointed out that there are really only a limited number of decent plots to make a good play (or movie). Most of them require a death or murder to create a strong drama. In the entertainment capital, so much time and attention is given to death and murder in television and film that on hot days the place buzzes like a plague of locusts. People there are as obsessed with it as they are about sex and glamour. What good Hollywood picture doesn't have a murder or at least a handgun in it? The whole valley itself can't naturally support human life. Most of the time it's a desert fire-trap. On the right day from the hills, it really looks like hell.

It's no drooling wonder that West Coast gangsta rap works like an ambulance chase, on the lookout for the next victim to make money on. Murder sells. From Iceberg Slim, who wrote about his tough life as a pimp in the fifties, to Ice T, who claims him as an influence, LA was never really about The Beach Boys and Fun With Archie. It's a scary-

35

ass place when you see it with its pants down.

The Lincoln took us to Malibu where I fell in love with a tattooed punk who worked at a nudist colony. We played in the sand. But she felt nothing for anyone after her brother had been shot at close range in Venice. The Lincoln took us past Marilyn Monroe's ashes and past the house where Charles Manson became an overnight sensation. We played mix-tapes through four broken speakers. Easy listening and Mexican border music.

Arthur Lyman, Los Gavilanes, Tijuana Brass

They had me on the casting couch, I'm ashamed to say. The Lincoln took us to Burbank studios for auditions with young, shameless, grovelling actors, clawing, upstaging and out-shouting one another for the roles. "You in the back, we can't see or hear you..." I stood up on the casting couch and showed them a glimpse of my vortex. No call back. Another movie about young Americans who drive across the country killing people. No thanks.

Kalifornia, True Romance, Pulp Fiction... I stopped going to the pictures for years after that summer. Aristotle didn't mention mixing tragedy with sneering irony, stringing together coolisms and sexed-up vampire sluts, as being the best formula for good drama. The list of plots didn't include popping your brother just because you're too stupid to know better. That's a modern American plot.

The Lincoln drove us happy stoners to Forest Lawn Memorial Park in Glendale next.

Martin Denny, Yma Sumac, Los Lobos

There, are buried many of the famous: Walt Disney, W. C. Fields, Humphrey Bogart... and it's such a cemetery as would challenge the puke reflex of even the most cynical man.

Forest Lawn is a theme park for the dead. One can be buried in Graceland, an Elvis-themed plot, or Babyland, which is for babies, in the shape of a heart. One can hear Tchaikovsky playing softly over one's grave for all eternity. And one can be buried under a replica of Michelangelo's *David*, or under Homer or Zeus. Some people even get married in one of the many themed fake antique chapels. Ronald Reagan was married in the Wee Kirk O' the Heather. Tourists and mourners ride around together in happy little golf carts. Read *The Loved One* by Evelyn Waugh for full effect.

The Lincoln took us through the village of homeless in their tarpaulin shelters in Downtown LA and down to Babe and Ricky's blues bar in South Central. The once glittering strip where early R&B, jump, jive, rock'n'roll and all America's best black music thrived and prospered under flashing lights is now a buzzard's lunch. It's derelict and deadly for a small white bluesman to go near. No effort made to preserve it. Fucked over and forgotten.

Etta James, Louis Jordan, James Brown, Marlena Shaw

And on and on past abandoned art deco hotels, forgotten cinemas and ballrooms, vacant lots and bodies. But when the Lincoln returned home for the last time to the Magic Hotel on Franklin, the vortex yawned and sucked me into the lobby where the carpet had turned red and detectives coolly asked me if I knew how George the night clerk had been shot dead for no apparent reason.

The hotel staff had been like a reluctant family to me for a long time. The next day, the Lincoln took us to the funeral. The service was in Turkish. Catholic. George was buried in Forest Lawn Memorial Park. I couldn't hear his wife and children grieving over the sound of the eight-lane freeway by George's head. Borderland. One can be buried by a freeway for a fraction of the price. Men in yellow hard hats bulldozed the earth in on top of him.

After near-death on an exit ramp, some riots and mudslides, the work dried up and I left town. The car's engine seized up shortly after. Kyle has assumed responsibility for keeping it alive. Apparently he's revived it now and it's calling me back to what makes America and all of us so afraid of death. Los Angeles de Muertos.

A YOUNG BRANCH TAKES ON ALL
THE BENDS ONE GIVES IT

Issue 15, March 2008

People often ask me if I have any words of advice for young people. I do have several things to say.

1. Stay the fuck out of my yard. Your candy wrappers and empty beer tins don't impress anyone, and if no one is impressed with you, you are unloved, and that will start to feel awful. You'll get sick and die before you are old enough to get revenge on the world you so want to pollute.

2. People over 40 are perfectly capable of rocking out, but usually choose to sell garbage to young people for the cash instead. I know I'll make a children's record when the first bad reviews come in.

3. Don't buy anything being sold to you because you're a young person. Pop music by 17-year-old girls is manufactured to get your money and will leave you as hungry as you would be having eaten a little bag of Walker's potato chips. Fat businessmen want to sell soft porn and deodorant by convincing you you're ugly and sexless. Be offended. Seek revenge through the right channels, however.

4. Don't attack innocent people on the street who aren't part of the plot to sell you garbage.

5. Avoid normality and all those who claim to be normal.

6. Women are not more beautiful than men. That's a myth. Part of the plot to make you buy things. Put down the shiny beauty magazine and actually look at James Dean. You're never gonna look that good so don't be so fucking vain.

7. Don't follow the advice of old cranks who aren't normal and contradict themselves.

Round about 1962, a crank named Dave was boarding a

Greyhound bus in the Canadian Rockies headed south for Berkeley, California. He wore a long trenchcoat he'd brought back from the war. He had a subversive-looking beard, a .22 revolver in his pack and a Jack Kerouac novel in his pocket. Surprisingly, they wouldn't let him across the border.

But it wasn't the gun, the beard, or the beat novel that held him back. It was the cranky abnormal things he was saying about a man's right to find work wherever he felt like it. They didn't want a dispossessed man coming in, working and giving advice to their college students.

He played Fats Waller.

They played Lawrence Welk.

8. Don't join any interest groups or fraternities in order to belong. If you must put on a costume and stand about like a goth, a greaser or a new raver, don't apply it permanently. There are 90 years of pop music and several hundred years of fashion to choose from. Your first choice will be foolish. You can't remove a spider's web tattoo from your face.

9. Never hitchhike alone.

Pairs of eyes in the trees following us. Wolves, for chrissake. What have I got myself into? My pal hacked his hand while chipping ice on a glacier in the Canadian Rockies. We're hitching to the nearest city where they can repair it. We urinate in the snow so the beasts will know us better and we talk about music.

We're dispossessed. Our older brothers and sisters had all the glory in the sixties and early seventies. Punk has already mutated into American hardcore. We talk about the early R&B and what never made it up to Canada. We had some of the first Walkmans and some fine hashish.

I played UB40's *Signing Off*.

He played *Abbey Road*, side 2.

I played James Cotton.

He played Hank Williams.

Everybody's trying to tell you what to do when you're young.

39

It's important not to listen sometimes. I left my buddy in a nice hospital bed and continued through the Midwest where the most insane and inbred people cruise the highways looking for hitchhikers to fuck up.

My first ride was with the Jonestown family who drove me against my will to a huge suburban superchurch for prayers. I ran from that opportunity.

My second ride was the eczema man. I politely enquired after his health. He crudely offered to suck me off. You can't punch a fellow until after he stops the car and the door is open.

The next ride was a long night drive.

"You see the lights followin' us?"

"Uh, yeah."

"That's one of my boys. I have several of 'em workin' for me on my ranch. Wayward youth with no place to go. I'm thinkin' that maybe you need a place to go."

"Uh, no, I'm alright."

"You know I once killed a man with my bare hands. Punched him so hard in the guts that I was able to pull on his spine from the front."

Of all the helpful old lunatics to ride with, I was the most curious about this one. But I passed on this offer too, thinking to myself that I've got to find my own way. Not join any Mountain man cults, pimp myself out to peeling queers or fall into any superchurches until I'd seen a little more of our grand country.

Now, decades later, dear children, I realise that I have become the dispossessed, peeling fanatic with his truck waiting to find lost young souls to fuck up. No one really asks perverted old bluesmen for their advice. But people listen politely and sometimes pay us to go away. It makes one bitter sometimes.

10. See item 1.

Me and some crazy friends worked in the hotels long enough to buy an old wreck. Drove back through the prairies listening to Neil. By the time I saw the herd of bison crossing the road, we were in the middle of it. Just parked there surrounded by other heavy brown beasts watching the sun come up. It was a cool scene. Man, where were you?

"My dad sent me to law school."

11. Eat the rich. They taste like organic free-range chicken.

THE SKY'S NO LESS BLUE BECAUSE
A BLIND MAN CAN'T SEE IT

Issue 16, May 2008

You wanna know what really racks me off? Pseudo-socialist opinionated squeaky Canadian comfortable sweater-wearing assholes who can't keep their snide pious comments to themselves. Heh heh heh. In this story, sweet revenge is had. Socialist policies and multicultural-ism have their place in the big picture, but until you have a culture and hard history of your own, it's best to keep your loud mouth shut about the affairs of the world.

A magic and wild civilisation has evolved just out of reach of the American marketing machine. Like a petri dish experiment gone right for a change, the people of Cuba have grown strong and interesting while much of Western culture slides into decadence and narcissism.

A simple recipe: lots and lots of African slaves, brutal Spanish colonial repression and bloodshed for 200 years, a dash of Chinese, spice with gorgeous colonial and art deco architecture, then isolate with only 1950s technology for 60 years. Now open cautiously.

The bench where we sit drinking rum and smoking strong cigarettes is once again surrounded with bodies and bottles as the sky lights up and the pounding heat of the day returns. At my feet are shakers and butts and broken tambourines. By my side are dead batteries and a portable amplifier. On the next bench my personal guide, his slightly Chinese eyes looking sleepy.

The police have been watching all night and are tired, but satisfied. The fountain comes to life in Plaza Dolores in Santiago de Cuba, perhaps the most musical place in the world. For five nights, this bench has been the best spot in town for a dance, drink and some very weird music. These bums I call my friends are perhaps the happiest bums on the planet. Their medical bills are well covered and the set of teeth on the bench opposite is expertly made.

Back home in London, the bums smell much worse and will steal your socks and have no rhythm. Cuba is safer, a thousand times more peaceful, and music rings out everywhere. My friends in Ska Cubana have sent me here and set me up in a good Casa Particular (B&B) and shown me a glimpse of the good life.

My first prostitute was Angelo. He wouldn't admit he's a *jinetero*, but he's a good one. Of course we didn't exchange fleshy contact, but it was a healthy reciprocal arrangement whereby he lived off me for a couple days in return for his 'friendship' and local drinking knowledge. This practice of helping tourists is illegal in Cuba, as it often leads to marriage and emigration, but with my big hairy Cuban hombre there wasn't a danger. The police watch the bars as we leave separately and walk 10 metres apart. It's an art.

He took me to Casa de la Trova, where the crowd was up on the tables in the afternoon. Seventy-five-year-old toothless cigar hags blew me kisses through the bars on the window as I blew solos with an eleven-piece band. We went to club Artex to hear traditional Son de Santiago and the UNEAC to see wild ancient dance performances in the courtyard. He delivered plastic bags full of old, scarred and grime-covered 45s of the early mambo kings. They cost me dearly.

Then I met Wilfredo and fell in love again. He was my waiter under the stars. He took us by a smoke-belching 1951 Chevrolet to the cascades with Olga the buxom Estonian girl, a bucket of beer and freshly caught fish. The money I paid him went towards a pig (whom I met briefly), which was to be killed and eaten that New Years Eve (while I would be playing at The George Tavern in London). The simplest transactions, if they can't be measured and taxed by governments, become illegal. Friends become hustlers and criminals in the guidebooks and police reports.

And they were always there watching. Different shirts for different policing duties. Dark blue shirts were there to protect the tourists. They were comforting. But there were others outside my Casa Particular who recorded my arrival and departure and weren't so welcoming. It was after the first night that they arrived.

Men, women, children and homos (they hang out in the square too, bless them) were gathered around, contentedly listening to modern blues music at The Bench. Some were singing along. A paranoid street artist was painting the scene. A cool, quiet, very black brother called Walter was to my right playing percussion. On the left a tall, intense, Latin-looking dude was seriously getting down. The children were all given plastic dinosaurs and art supplies to keep them from grabbing the controls.

But suddenly, The Canadian Asshole lurches through the crowd and screams: "Hey man, take that shit out of here, these beautiful people don't need your Western garbage coming in here and polluting their culture..."

Well, shit the bed, there was one helluva pregnant pause as everyone looked back and forth from me to the pious Canadian, and at the police who remained still and observant by the fountain, just conserving energy in the heat and amused by this development.

The moment was broken by the scary Latino to my left. He launched himself off the bench, fists in the air, and screamed vile abuse at the dumbfounded Canuck, who ducked and covered and was chased around the square. The Cuban returned, lit a smoke, and struggled in English to give a speech that went something like this:

"Mr Bluesman, you are our brother. You have come to Cuba to play for us this strange and wonderful music. We have never heard anything like it before. Nobody comes to Cuba to play music for the people in the street. From the bottom of my heart, I wish to thank you and welcome you and tell you that we will protect you and you can stay on this bench and play music and drink rum for as long as you want."

The people were satisfied with his serious speech. I was especially pleased and we all began another dance as the Canadian shouted from the other side of the fountain. The police rocked their heads to the rhythm that Walter laid down in the Afro Cubano style. Teenage tough guys grabbed the mic and rapped in Spanish. The bums were fighting over the tambourine. Angelo procured another bottle of rum and Cuba will never be the same, but always the same, as the doors swing open to let in the air and the riff-raff.

TEEN SPIRIT PISSES ALL OVER
THE GOOD-HUMOURED MAN

Issue 17, Summer 2008

There are two kinds of people in the world: those who piss on the toilet seat and those who don't. Radio 1 and their team of energetic DJs and media graduates have the difficult task of entertaining the seat pissers, and still trying to live up to an astonishing history of great British music. How do they wade through the yellow floods of youth and move on from the mountains of wet grampers?

In England, they speak of the weather, and they piss on the seat. All seats at popular music concerts in England are pissed on — equally by women as they are by men. Radio 1 organise concerts by supporting bands who in turn encourage drinking and recklessness and general snide behaviour, and the piss just flows and flows. It's an unfortunate by-product of the music industry.

It isn't so bad in France, Germany, the Netherlands or Belgium. Spain and Italy are pretty pissy, but that's partly because of the British tourists.

In the rolling hills and farmlands of Austria, vanloads of young hippies strummed guitars and tended their campfires and waited for the evening concert to begin. There were three bands on the bill. The Yardbirds, The Troggs, and Son of Dave. There was to be no sleep that night again, after so many nights of sold-out UK club gigs and terrible travelling. This night I was playing with Old People, who rock without fear of consequence.

Backstage, I approached the largest and coolest-looking old sixties bastard, and held out my hand. He had a purple tie-dye on and beads. "I'm the nurse with the Yardbirds," he said. Chris Dreja later explained to me that he had had his gall bladder removed only two weeks before.

45

Jeezuz. He also talked about his love for a portable digital radio. I asked if he listened to BBC Radio 1. He looked at me as though I'd just spat in his sherry. I apologised.

It was an honour to see an ancient posse of British moguls on stage right as I blasted out post-modern blues and pulled the hippy girls onto the stage. They came onstage, stole a maraca and disappeared.

Chris Trogg, the guitarist, did NOT piss on the toilet seat in my dressing room, though he used it a couple times. He is a Great Pirate of rock and I admire him. The question became: will I get any sleep if I try to find the hippy chick who took my maraca? So many tents to rattle. Or will I get any sleep if I go with this pirate into town for a pub crawl?

A cool old person is a joy to be around. Sometimes they can't help it when the pee-pee sprays out, but it's entirely forgivable. I gave Honeyboy Edwards one of my handkerchiefs the other day. He's 92 and sometimes needs to suddenly water while he walks. He was around when Little Walter was showing off the new Cadillac that Chess Records bought him and Muddy Waters went wild with envy. Or something like that. It's hard to make out what Honeyboy says sometimes. He speaks Delta bluesman. And only has a couple beers after a show.

But The Troggs are 30 years younger and spry as foxes in comparison. I chose to forget my maraca and, as always, followed the music and the booze rather than the girl with no social graces. Chris made us drink and chain-smoke in a rock bar until 5am before our flight three hours later. In order to impress a pirate of this magnitude, it's necessary to move something very, very heavy such as an old sewing machine against his hotel room door. Maybe he'd be impressed with my hernia.

No sleep. The stench of cigarettes and service station schnapps. Oh dear, I'm sitting next to Reg Trogg on the plane. Mad genius. Completely likeable. He wrote 'Wild Thing' and plenty of other hits including 'Love Is All Around You', recently made famous by Wet Wet Wet (ha ha ha).

It must be said, Reg is a complete crop circle of a man. He talked about his new film starring Ant and Dec, called *Alien Autopsy*. He talked about Mayan burial chambers and mystic medicines and 2012 doomsday theories until my head was hard and gaping like the ancient stones of Easter Island. I asked if he's started collecting tinned goods yet. He said that most tinned goods expire in 2011, so it's too early to stock up. I pulled down the eyeshades and passed out.

I dreamt of Paul McCartney in a grass skirt. He did a DJ set on Radio 1 not long ago. And he had Dave Grohl from the Foo Fighters on stage to drum to Beatles and Wings singalongs when he played in Liverpool. Radio 1 like to play the Foo Fighters, but they don't play much Paul McCartney these days. I wonder how his bladder is holding out. He sure played a good concert.

Radio 1 don't play much Honeyboy Edwards, or Little Walter, or Muddy Waters, or The Troggs, or The Yardbirds. They play Adele, and Foals, and Vampire Weekend. They keep things VERY YOUNG AND ENERGETIC! Good for them.

Meanwhile, England is becoming renowned for its sour, soaked rock'n'roll concerts, its vile festival toilets, and its shit-smeared Barfly venues. Maybe they will put Neil Diamond music on heavy rotation and the ladies will learn to put their used tampons into the toilet rather than on the floor. Backstage at Africa Express in Liverpool, no sleep, tampons on the floor. Imagine the bogs at last year's Brit Awards!

When you're not under 30 anymore, youth culture just appears boring. It smells of wee. Didn't you learn anything from your parents? They rocked harder than you ever will. Or maybe I've got it all backwards. I can't keep up with all these new-fangled anal-fisting drug remixes. Back in the nineties, we just had regular-fisting drug mixes. Must sleep soon. Young people taking over... broken glass everywhere. Same as it ever was. When do we move forward?

CHINA, UNLIKE GLASS AND
REPUTATION, IS HARD TO CRACK

Issue 18, October 2008

You can dance with their daughter, but there's an iron chastity belt downstairs with the key at the bottom of a tank of electric eels. You may submerge your head and fight the eels with your teeth to retrieve the key. Shanghai is a very romantic city.

Waiting at the airport, huddled in a sleepy drunken group, the nineties pop stars waited in fear for over two hours as their work visas were processed by the tour manager and Chinese officials. Airport staff in green workers' uniforms, complete with the little red star on the hat, glided by, eating with chopsticks from steaming bowls of noodles. In the public washrooms, a rusty tin can on the back of the toilet held a burning joss stick. That ever-present institutional mint green paint and bad fluorescent lighting made it obvious that you were in communist China. In fact, this was one of the first Western bands to be invited. Some Canadian promoter had done the unimaginable and opened the door for Western acts there in 1996. The West came roaring in like savages. Again.

At the Portman Shangri-La, it would arrive and from there it would plan the attack. Shanghai is now an overwhelming forest of shiny skyscrapers. But just 12 years ago, the Portman hotel was one of the few tall, decadent buildings; a luxury hotel, regarded by the locals with awe and disgust.

From the 20th floor, you could see the whole city rising up and being built over. Cranes and, unbelievably, bamboo scaffolding were just beginning to churn out glass and steel towers that the West had taken for granted for decades.

Beside the hotel was a bar (run by more Canadians) called the

American Bar; kind of ordinary with spicy wings and a big screen TV. We tumbled in and drank more in the hope of getting a good sleep at night and reversing our body clocks. It doesn't work: one just finds the power to drink endlessly, then has a broken sleep, then the hangover is a nightmare set among tanks of eels and chickens being plucked. You would expect a coffee shop, but there's no English printed or spoken anywhere. Seething chaos on bikes.

The Chinese eat everything. They laugh and slap you on the back and push more shots of snake bile into your hand. The roof leaks into a bowl of shiny black winkles, and there is good cheer and dangerous merriment. More wild than their Japanese enemies offshore. They talk with their hands like Italians. Even the cripples must work and smile, delivering refrigerators on hand-pedalled bicycles. I promised I'd return to live in it, but I'm weak now. Wouldn't take LSD anymore in middle age either. Thanks anyway.

The problem began when the promoter told the pop stars that before we received the final go-ahead from the Ministry of Culture to perform at a sold-out concert in two days, they would like to see a video. In the days before the internet could deliver that, a tape had to be flown from North America at great cost. It would be last minute. Until permission was given, the authorities sent men with newspapers and sunglasses to follow us and make sure we didn't burst into songs of rebellion.

If we could crack the Chinese market, we'd be billionaires! If we could get them all smoking cigarettes and opium, they could fund our old boys' club for generations! If only. But the Chinese won't fall for that again and they'll make it much more difficult now. Now they have plenty of bloodthirsty businessmen of their own to capitalise on the party. Warner Bros. are pulling out! See, the panic hit whitey in the wallet!

The old man was no hustler. Slow as a snail. I asked him directions and was surprised by his English. He had worked as an interpreter for a bank for 30 years and was still dirt poor. If I bought him dinner, he'd take me wherever I wanted to go. He ordered a simple and delicious meal, I demanded ballroom dancing, he took me to his regular hang-out and I danced with old Chinese women to a sedated, synthetic-sounding swing band. We talked of the cultural revolution and *Madame Butterfly*. He was happy that they were allowed to play the old music again. I returned to the American Bar for one more drink with the crew. The place was an animal house. Our whole entourage was snot-faced. The owner was filling up trays of shots on the house. The men with newspapers and shades were watching with pained expressions.

I was told the videotape had arrived that evening. The ministry of culture watched it. Unfortunately, some fool had given them the wrong video: a farcical thing, banned by MTV, which had cost 50 grand US, starring the lead from the movie *Kids* and featuring scenes of his teeth being pulled out with pliers. With a simple shake of the head, the Chinese decided we were a threat to their enormous population and had cancelled the concert. I raised the tiger urine to my lips and leapt from the balcony on to the dancefloor, a five-metre drop. Then I saw her.

She came down a stairway and we stared at each other. She spoke first: "Where have you *been*?" I said: "I'm sorry I'm late." I took her in my arms and knew she was perfect. She was from Frisco. She was a journalist, had a Sigourney Weaver toughness and drank like a soldier. We kissed vulgarly in a barber chair at the bar. She tilted the chair back and said something in Cantonese to the bartender. He mixed a drink in my mouth. She drank it. Then we reversed positions. Shanghai is a very romantic place. This continued until she lurched aggressively into a cab, leaving me with an illegible phone number. My heart has been suspended ever since.

At five in the morning, the boulevard outside the towering hotel fills up with old couples who quietly do Tai Chi and dance to swing music and schmaltz. It's surreal. I watched for a while and cried uncontrollably until one of the crew put me to bed, where I lay laughing until unconsciousness.

In the press scrum which I woke up to, we were instructed to say that there had never been a concert to play. Orwellian. No concert. Don't attempt to explain why.

"So, you are excited to play big concert in Shanghai tonight?"

"There is no concert."

The reporters stared blankly, then moved on to other questions, understanding immediately what had happened. Barely even a knowing look was looked. Fear. Government. Prison.

The truly adventurous go to China and survive. A complete reverse polarity. It's a wild frontier. The characters in the American Bar were cast in iron. A Texan complete with hat and loud mouth. What the hell was he doing in China? Pig hooves. He bought all the hooves to make film out of them. Millionaire in three years. Nice guy, actually.

The artists who were dodging the system and trying to do something political, the journalists with the sense of a mosquito flying towards a major artery, and the people running or hiding from something, all had the courage to move to a madhouse where the signs and sounds are indecipherable. What it takes to move from Ipswich to Hackney versus what it takes to move from Smallville to Big Chinatown.

The Chinese want a lot from the West now, but on their own terms. Control. The grinning face with the gun poking in the ribs. As much as the Olympics opened them up, they shut the ugly in the dungeons. The hypocrisy of advertising reaches new lows with a pretty girl lip-syncing, while the ugly girl sings from her cage. They learned how to do it from America. They will do it better. I'm too weak and hungover now to do anything but watch. Decadent Westerner.

A PARASITE BY ANY OTHER NAME
STILL SMELLS AS FOUL

Issue 19, December 2008

Know thine enemy. Name the brute. Adam came down from the trees to name the beasts and so became master over them. Our ability to reason puts us above those creatures that just act on instinct. And so I say: you are the Greedy Whore!

A little poke around and we can see where the blockage in the system is. Though the internet has opened up a world for interesting and great music to move around in, the power of radio over people's minds and wallets is still supreme. The hit machine is as strong as it ever was.

At time of writing, the BBC Radio 1 A and B playlists can be broken up into the following categories: music you might like, music you might not like, and over-polished works of cynics that revolt me and must be destroyed. Something is exhausting the music biz like a huge tapeworm. If we hold a steak by the ass end of it, she will come out and we can kill her.

Out of 35 tunes on their playlist, 13 are by female acts. Every one of those tunes was written and produced by teams of experts, mostly men, hell-bent on taking tonnes of money from teenagers. Except one, written by Bob Dylan, which Adele tries to sing. Yes, a third of the playlist is constantly held by a handful of hit-making cartels and the puppets are the Girls on Parade.

Name them. Xenomania: a few men and women who write and produce songs for Sugababes, Girls Aloud, Kylie Minogue, Cher, Texas, Miley Cyrus, Alesha Dixon and many more. Max Martin is another who, like some mad shit machine, made the biggest hits for Britney Spears, Pink, Katy 'I-Kissed-The-Devil's-Scrotum' Perry, Celine Dion, Backstreet Boys, 'N Sync, Bon Jovi and more. There are also writers and producers like Eg White and Mark Ronson who wait outside the Brit School gates for the likes of Duffy, Adele, Amy Winehouse and the many who are scheduled to take their place.

We might ask, what is the BBC doing, relying so heavily on produced pop acts? Who is to blame for all the fatty build-up that's clogging up the rock'n'roll arteries? Is there a backroom deal? Is it the record companies, the radio programmers fresh out of media school, the kids who buy the shit, or is it the pop divas? Hey bub, a girl's gotta make a living! Well, not if I can bloody help it. She's holding me down with her stiletto poking in my windpipe and I don't like that. Unless I've asked for it.

She stared up at me from the front row and never let up with those icy Russian eyes and athlete's figure. She moved her hips too slowly to call it dancing. So the middle-aged bluesman chased her out of the crowd, and it didn't take much convincing to get her to join me in the parade, watch the fireworks over the Thames, drink rum and dance on a boat to the Cumbia Kid playing old Latin vinyl till 4am. She said she was a singer.

She wanted information and purred up against me for it. She wanted to know where I went for nightlife in town. She found me exotic. I suggested dinner. I thought she was joking when she said I couldn't afford her tastes.

It's a small percentage who understand that a diamond is worthless unless you believe in it. Primitive tribes used gems and stones as currency. The king had the most. It was simple. But today, most people still see gold and platinum as intrinsically good stuff to own and wear. Like stapling £10,000 notes to your earlobes. That would probably catch on. It would be honest, anyway.

She made me meet her for a drink in Green Park behind the Royal Academy. I'd managed to avoid those streets up till then: Gucci, Lacoste, Cartier, Gianfranco Zola. Cecconi's. She was at the bar drinking champagne. The staff knew her by name. The tables were full of suits and diamonds. Nobody was smiling. These are serious times for money people.

Tonight, the thought of Phil Spector's shaking hands and terrifying humour are keeping me awake. How many girl groups did he create with his songs and sonic genius? From The Ronettes to John Lennon, he was unstoppable and demented. Music was like revenge to him. I strongly identify and would enjoy gunplay with him someday! I sleep and dream of sitting on a dock with him and shooting at fish with high-powered rifles.

But ultimately we all prefer the real thing: a woman, not a girl, with her own song to sing. A woman who can belt it out like she means it, pound on a piano, and shake her bosom when the camera ain't there. A rare thing, brother.

The Russian Princess told me about her new recording advance. I gasped. She turned her collar up to come outside and smoke. Burberry. I said I didn't feel comfortable with all these rich people around. She said I was just jealous. I said let's walk over to Soho for a drink. She said she'd never been to Soho and doubted they'd have single malt whiskey there.

She turned me on and off like a lamp, the way media people do, suddenly talking over your shoulder or getting on the phone. You're just jealous, she said. I explained that I don't mind paying for excellent food, but I don't want most of the crap that rich people have. Talk to me when you're there, she said, and suddenly ordered a waiter to bring us some olives and more champagne. I said something childish and walked out.

I didn't know what to do! I bottled. Face-to-face with the tapeworm itself and I just ran. I went to the French House and drank wine until two tears came out. Then I was happy again. Then to Tricia's or one of the actor's bars, I don't remember. It's so hard to helplessly watch the bastards slide around inside her. Feels lonely out here sometimes, but that's where a good bluesman belongs, not inside with the backslappers. Though I might ask her to sing the chorus of this tune I'm humming...

IT'S TIME TO PICK THE WEAKEST
GATE AND SMASH THROUGH IT

Issue 20, March 2009

"Look ready to face the day," you fascist swine worshipper. Get out of bed and put on your gimp suit, the Nivea ad says. Look forward to the profits. If you spray this slick shit on your face, no one will smell the hungry stray you slept with last night while you were all coked up. If you wear this urban camouflage, no one will recognise you from the disco the night before. You can go about your booming business of buying and selling other people's hard work at great profit without any fear of being held responsible for their impoverished lives. Then you can come home with another faceless fashion whore and play her the songs you learned to play at college. "What men want." Indeed.

These are exciting times. Capitalism is facing some heavy scrutiny, but it's by no means weakened despite the economy drunkenly riding a unicycle on a high wire. It's fun to try and figure out who's gonna profit from an economic collapse. Someone always profits from someone else's loss. When huge amounts of dough seem to disappear, interesting things happen. But, like energy, money isn't created or lost. It just moves and changes and big explosions go off. Where is the lady, where's the lady?

These times are not without hope. With so much scrutiny, and with so many people re-assessing what it is to make money, we can see the poker face of capitalism and we can see that some of the huge profits earned through institutionalised gambling were from marked decks. Hopefully some of the money will be put back on the table and the cheaters will be marked. Then we can start the dirty game all over again.

The man in this Nivea ad (not the poor witless model, but the character) is not a teacher. He isn't a fisherman or bartender or dentist or doctor. He is a young businessman. Possibly an estate agent. He earns a percentage. He wins when others lose. He looks like Mark Ronson. I'm sure it wasn't intentional.

The guitar in the background represents his youth. The woman in the bed is nice to have had, but most importantly, with his suit, the smug little bastard is telling us to prioritise the professional life. We can have our childish rock'n'roll and our bimbos, but the money is where it's at. (Notice ties are getting thinner again! Fat businessmen are out of style. The look should be slimmer now. Shows that you know how to budget. A more vertical line. Trim. Times are tight. Profit comes only to those who are quick on their feet and ruthless as fuck.)

For two decades, businessmen have been seeing themselves as rock stars up in first class; the travelling, the shades, the jewellery, the gadgets and loose women. The big problem is that some confused people in the music business try to compete with these pinheads. The men and women who own music retail chains, record companies, video channels, guitar manufacturers, publishing companies, radio stations, MySpace share-holders, and established shiny music magazines, all probably have one thing in common: they enjoy music, and are clever enough to make a living working with what they love. But if a line were to be drawn in the sand, which side would they stand on? Music over here, finance over there. It's a tricky business selling art, advertising love, or capitalising on youthful spirit. It's become impossible to tell the city man and the A&R man apart. Terrifying.

These times are volatile. Money doesn't accurately reflect work done or energy expended. It's not a fair measure of real worth. But it's the only measure some people understand, and they measure you by your wealth. Money is practical. I can't exchange a box of CDs for a train ticket. In fact, I can't exchange a box of CDs for anything these days. So when huge amounts of money get hijacked, the *surface* worth of everything changes and that makes for some very upset and defensive people. They can go off like rockets. But true worth is not flammable. Some of us don't have to worry. A good bluesman doesn't have to worry.

Nivea moisturiser isn't anything more than rubbing paraffin on an ugly face. My doctor prescribes me the good stuff, with quite simple ingredients in it. The popular brands are designed to make you smell pretty, feel nice and moist for a while, but then they wear off so you need to buy more. That beautiful young male model in the ad may find himself scratching and wheezing in a few years as the allergies and asthma set in. Then the Nivea won't be worth a fart. It takes axle grease to keep the skin from falling off all over your date's dinner when your immune system fights your own hide. I could recommend some powerful steroids to help him with this.

I'd like to be the poster boy for steroid creams. In the bed beside me there'd be a big strong Danish gal rolling a joint, some old 45s and a little turntable. I'd still be in elegant pyjamas I inherited from my grandfather. The slogan would be: "If only everyday were like this." The campaign would be called: "Life's more worth living with the help of Western medicine." This won't make sense to most people. But it needs to be said in case somebody understands it. He or she won't feel so alone in their madness.

I passed this damned Nivea ad and became obsessed with it while on the way to Paris to perform on French telly. Then, on the train, I fell asleep and dreamed this dream:

I was eating lunch in Terminus Nord. The phone rang. It was my agent. They wanted me in a Levi's ad wearing the new blue jeans that I'd designed. Tonight. "How much?" I asked. "10,000," he said. "No way, not for under 100 grand."

The jeans I had designed were high-waisted, dark blue denim, or black, with small belt-loops for a skinny belt, or buttons for braces. The concealed change pocket is right up above the belt in the lining. They have two pleats and are baggy as zoots with a turn-up at the bottom. The dangling lucky dice wallet chain is sold separately. Together with a simple, old thin-strap undershirt and paperboy cap, the return to the 1940s' American ghetto is put in tune with the youth of today. The return to classics brings back long lost American pride. Tattoos and diamond necklaces keep the look glamorous and dangerous. The 'homey-chip' in the Levi's tag lets our friends know where we are... or we can set it to private for when we're crime-ing.

"They want you to model them. It's perfect timing for the album release. The publicity will be huge and worth millions in album sales. You should probably just take the 10 grand they're offering."

"But Levi's are loaded! And what about their sweatshops in Canada? Everybody knows they treat the natives like slaves and just pay them with booze and cigarettes."

"Listen, it isn't your job to set the work standard for the company — just design the jeans and wear 'em for the camera."

"Okay, I'll let you call this one, Harvey, but I'm not gonna let them tell me how to accessorise, and you can warn them ahead of time about that. I'll be on the toilet and not taking any calls until 6pm. Ciao."

Then the French waiter purposely pours scalding soupe à l'oignon all over my crotch and I knew the jeans were ruined... I woke up screaming. My pecker was burning from the Oil of Olay.

This moment in time is crucial. There is confusion in their camp. We need to pick the least fortified gate and crash it. Then we find the guns and melt them. Then we find the gold and put it back in the ground. Then we make the bastards play music for *us* while we relax for a bit. Softer. No, not like that, I'm trying to make love to your wife... Yes, that's a sexy chord change. Now sing something about the old days before advertising made liars of us all.

THEY NEVER LEARN, BUT THE SAVAGES
MUST BE TAUGHT A LESSON

Issue 21, May 2009

That evening on my adman phone, I'd managed to complete a contract with Hugo Boss and Davidoff cigars and I was celebrating, you know? We're opening a theme park on one of the lesser-known Chanel Islands, directly above the Channel Tunnel. An elevator shaft is being dug to bring lucky contest winners up from the tunnel and pop them out right by the Stooge 'o Whirl ride! And upon producing a smoking hot improvised branding iron made from coat hangers and a Burberry umbrella, the room froze and the heavies shut the door and surrounded me. Maybe I'd taken the gag too far.

The darlings of the Australian Big Day Out Festival after-parties this year were The Flaming Bitch Puffers. They were swarthy veterans with mean-looking roadies, and completely tattooed from head to toe. Everyone wanted a photograph snapped with them. I was pushed into position near them once but there were magazine clippings on my face and marker pens up my nose and I wasn't really on top of what was happening.

In the performers' hotel in Adelaide, I think it was, the Puffers dimmed the lights in the super presidential puffer suite and put the heavies on the door. All the Chardonnay was in their control. They locked in all the best young women so the party downstairs was scant. I was just gonna give up on the evening because nobody wanted to talk about my Chanel Island when I found myself bum-steered into the lion's den.

Now most festivals are dull, dull, dull. The music is only part of the problem. Burlesque and cabaret have returned and actually provide some real entertainment, but that's still not enough to excuse hundreds

of thousands of drunk young genital heads in a field. The Lilyworld
stage at the Big Day Out festival in Australia tries to help. The festival
runs six shows in three weeks, with many Big Days Off for the rock
stars to play with each other. The gang of crazies who run Lilyworld
were hired 17 years ago as an "ambience team" to help make the festival
a more interesting experience. Very difficult work. I was hired to
perform in Lilyworld and help out. I was led into a sea of black t-shirted
rock bands, drunken V-chested surfers, Barbie girls on ecstasy, daily
temperatures of 28-42 degrees, and I struggled to stay amused.

Now, rock'n'roll is supposed to be a bit unpredictable and on the
road dramatic tales occur when things go wrong, but not too wrong, or
it's not funny. I feared someone would now lose an eye. The heavies are
advancing.

"This is my brand," I said. "It's the Son of Dave branding iron. I
won't use it as a weapon so please don't be alarmed. But I wanted to
offer the chance of a lifetime to some lucky contestant to be the first to
have this fantastic brand put onto their skin. I've just been on the phone
with my manager and it looks like we've just got the new single into a
Rack Daniel's advert. I'm celebrating. Anyone want to be branded? It
only takes a second and I have some antiseptic." I held up the blue
bubble bath.

How had I progressed to this dangerously weird gag from relative
sanity? Two weeks earlier, DJ Christo handed me a tall cool Trance
Juice as the sun went down in Byron Bay on another day off.

"Last month we started a wave in Goa?" he said. "Pure trance. We
lined up the bass bins at sunset, pointed them east. The wave is gonna be
here in an hour. It's a sundown mix. It's gonna wash all the dishes for
us."

Christo and I laughed late into the night until the Malcolm Ecstasy
gag, then turned in.

The next morning he hands me trance wear catalogues that he's
mysteriously sourced over night. I am firm with him. "Christo, my
room was full of Japanese business men last night all singing jazz remix
versions of every Christmas carol we could remember. We finished the

contract. The ad is done. It's a jazz remix day for sure."

"What? You can't do that! I've taken an anti-gag changing pill. Trance will never die!"

"The future's in ads and brand name remixes of Chardonnay and Pat Metheny, Christo, it's gonna be a blue mix!"

The others are looking at us in wonder. Duckpond is happy as usual and drawing on his shoes. Larry slaps me on the back and takes me aside: "Ah buddy, you went far out with Christo last night, didn't you? But we need you on gag duty on the airplane, you know?"

I eat another half a goof cake but don't tell him about the equestrian pictures I intend to fill the airplane WC with. He's happy today, too. Wearing a nice blue sunrise moo moo, his handsome face not too cracked to charm any stewardess. "Blue mix," I mutter and they put me on the plane.

I confuse and irritate the young-looking Arctic Monkey chap sitting next to me. He's trying to read *Catcher In The Rye* and relax. Seems very shy. Says he likes *The Stool Pigeon*, though, so he's highly intelligent. Ting Tings On The Radio. Pendulous, Bullet For My Firestarter and a hundred other weary rock stars stare, mildly amused as Heavy Gee steals the cheese platter and wine from business class and hands them around. Endurance, gags and idiot-speak at full volume. The suggestion of strange drugs and mystical knowledge is complete. They can tell we have the best party.

Some of the rock stars will make it to the Lilyworld stage by the end in Perth. But most won't. They'll wonder why they had such a boring tour. Rock'n'roll's a bit safe and predictable. Another tattoo won't make things more interesting. There's no room beside the Celtic knot and flaming pin-up girl. It's all paved over.

Sydney show. What a crowd! Pilled and boozed-up loogans everywhere. V-chested arsonists. The heatwave doesn't let up and the hyperactive music fans the flames. An assembly line of black t-shirts, rack and beer behind the main stage. A heavy presence of sniffer dogs keep the herb smoking grown-ups away. The BDO is struggling to stay cool. More concrete and fire on the horizon.

Son of Dave

In the oasis of Lilyworld, the Barbies in cheap sunnies crowd around to have bunnies drawn on their boobs by Duckpond, who has headphones made of airplane buns, black marker pen eyebrows, and a gin in his hand in the blazing afternoon sun. We hose them down for their own safety and they squeal and rub their chests against each other. Australia is filthy. Brits on a permanent holiday. Larry Chronic Junior shouts at them to line up for the sheep dip, they shout filth back, then jump in. It is spectacularly vulgar.

Everybody dances for hours to the pimpy beats and lunacy of Gee and Christo and Miles Cleret. Resenga the professional African Bushman is charming the mic and scaring the photographer with his elephant trunk. We will electrocute ourselves unless Benjy, the stage manager, separates the watering cans from the power cables. Long live these freaks who keep this stage going in the hope that at least one of the young men will learn how to enjoy good music, *Bill and Ben* costumes, and go-go girls without throwing up on himself.

So there I was, weeks of weird gags and crazy trips, holding up a homemade Burberry branding iron at the hotel party, flicking a Zippo and thinking it's funny. But predictably, no one grabbed the opportunity to have the thing thrust onto his already completely tattooed calf. I became very depressed. I took a swig of blue juice and blew a bubble. The guitarist told me to leave, while rewarding all the girls with champagne. Larry talked me down and smoothed things as usual. Thanks, big brother. I sloshed back to my room to do some handwashing, accustomed to this sort of anti-climax.

A last lunch in Perth with Duckpond. For 17 years he's been an unlikely leader of the only comic relief from main-stooge noise, not ever telling anyone what to do, exactly, just having a happy irresponsible time with some very stupid ideas that just might work. "Son of Dave, we've all been talking about you. You've been on 24-hour adman gag duty and been a fun part of the team. It would be great if you come back for Stoogefest 2010."

Christo puts down his coffee, lights an action-man cigarette and suggests, "We can recycle some jazz gags and make a fucked-ankle ad?

62

Done before, but it always works."

Hmmm. I ask, "Is it worth it? The V-chests are winning. They're starting fires. The girls are terribly confused and getting dumber. Will it always be so difficult to have fun?"

"Probably, buddy, but you seem to enjoy the challenge. And we enjoyed watching you stooge."

"Okay Duckpond, I'm in. The savages must be taught a lesson, even if they never learn."

"Ahhh, buddyyyy!"

THERE ARE FIVE RULES FOR ENSURING
A JOLLY GOOD BRITISH PUNCH-UP

Issue 22, Summer 2009

Bad party, April Financial Fools' Day, Bank, London, England. Still bitter. Still reading the papers. Makes ya bitter. Billy Bragg was there, with his buddy Kate Nash. Russell Brand was there and the Getting Wearing Flying Cape guy, too. Son of Dave was there but, unlike all these celebrities, I wasn't allowed out through the advancing police lines with the old "Do you know who I am?" because I wasn't famous enough. Don't riot cops read *The Stool Pigeon*? They fuckin' will.

The officer in charge of policing the G20, Commander Bob Broadhurst, said the day after the demo that the "overall mood" of the April 1st demonstration was good. But he added: "Unfortunately, small groups of protesters intent on violence mixed with the crowds of lawful demonstrators."

I know now that this above situation dictates that we lawful demonstrators be kicked, bullied, shoved, corralled, shocked and awed into complete submission by flanks of nervous, uninformed and occasionally brutal police in *RoboCop* costumes. Why was I kicked while cowering peacefully in the daffodils in front of the Bank of England? Why was I searched and spoken to like a criminal after waiting six hours to leave? It all made sense after this pathetic protester was arrested for having a two-inch keychain pocket knife, which ain't illegal, put in cuffs and driven to the cop shop. I was released without charge and thankfully closer to my final destination, Soho, where the drink never tasted so good, and the following simple explanation dawned on me.

From decades of practice with coal miners' strikes, labour rallies and race riots, they've learned how to contain and cook the books. And what more English expression than 'kettling' could there be? Bob turns up the heat in order to bring the party to a violent boil. Then they get the arrest numbers to justify the process and the demonstration deemed as unlawful by the larger public. Oh, it's so jolly clever.

Silly me. Being a foreigner, I didn't know the English way. I thought that if I went to a legal and organised demonstration I'd be allowed to grumble, pee on a bank, and leave without being kicked, searched and arrested. Wrong. Bad party. And that's what they want us to remember so we won't go back.

People, we need to have the procedure spelt out clearly. The English way is not to lay the rules out clearly and to pretend that it couldn't be clearer. To be held against their will with a minority of angry, young over-protesters was a shock to the majority of peaceful people who attended — young and old, straight and gay, naïve and educated, anonymous and not quite famous enough. The rules need to be clearly set.

This method of demonstration, which I witnessed and don't exaggerate much, needs to be posted as follows:

1. Protesters will be greeted and a strong but minimal police force will be seen providing reassurance, with the larger thugs being questioned, but nonetheless let in. Thousands of riot police, hundreds of vans and teams of dogs are kept just around the corners, out of sight as much as possible.

2. At the first sign of spray-paint and rowdiness, the area will be sealed off and the natural flow of protesters stopped. If there is no sign of rowdiness, some stooges will be sent in to create it. Then nobody gets in or out. (Although some more people may be let in if there is room, not knowing that they won't be let out. The elderly, likely to die, BBC camera crews, celebrities and the extremely posh will be allowed to leave at any time. Injured people may leave, but are to be searched and intimidated.)

3. The area will be gradually shrunk, five metres at a time, by sudden screaming walls of shielded, pushing-and-kicking police centurions. People may be given a two-second warning, at the officer's discretion, to run away before pushing and kicking and bludgeoning starts. Usual

practice is to scream "Move back!", "Move!", "Get out of the way!", and so on. Sometimes they say "please", which is very British. The people don't know where to go because, at the other end, is another line of advancing police saying the same things.

4. Once all the protesters are truly rattled, hungry, cold and tired, there will appear a narrow corridor against a long wall for them to be escorted down, one by one, 10 snarling dogs within one metre of biting. Then, when the protesters are in a terrifyingly small encampment, they will be coldly and accusingly questioned and searched. Anything at all which can be considered a weapon — a bicycle wrench, tools of any sort, gaffer tape, two-inch keychain pocket knives, forks — is grounds for arrest. Charges need not be pressed. There will be as many arrests as possible for the slightest thing, regardless of appearance, age, gender or manner.

5. The police will make the demonstration as unpleasant as possible without killing anyone. (Oh dear. The results of the third autopsy of poor Ian Tomlinson are being kept secret. The press has gone off the matter. Better, more bitter news has grabbed the headlines. But just wait...)

This is how things work. The system could even be improved if this game plan was publicised. Peaceful protests that turn violent could be avoided. We would then have peaceful ones and violent ones clearly separated. And, in fact, violent protests would likely become more popular, and the arrest numbers can go up, which works for both the police and the disgruntled British subjects. Like with the wars this government stirs up, the extremists become more easily vilified, and for the revolutionaries, there's a clearer path to martyrdom.

I see our police and state in a different light now. Well done chaps and tough ladies, mission accomplished. Well done England, we like a good riot. And here's to the boys who break windows: you've got guts! But remember, the police, politicians and big business depend on you to keep things confused and desperate. All day I saw them watching and laughing from the bank windows above. Actually laughing. Some saw them waving tenners. That's funny. The truth is funny. Let's see how funny things get in the coming years if the mob gets hungry.

Hey Kate, Billy, Cape Man, Russell, can I go to the next one with you guys? And can I leave with you too? Here's my number: 1. It's a little more expensive than other numbers, but it's easy to remember. Got it through Orange. French government owns most of Orange. I have connections there and their economy hasn't crashed as bad because their banks are better regulated. Their riots are even hairier, though.

NO CHOICE BUT TO GRIN AND BEAR IT, WHATEVER ISLAND YOU'RE ON

Issue 23, October 2009

On my summer holiday island, there are moss, spiders, ferns and three-metre wide, fifty-metre tall Douglas fir trees all around me. The campsite is quiet. After a beer and a flame-burnt sausage, I'll put everything except the tent into the trunk. If you don't do that, bears will come sniffing around and tear things up. When that happens, someone screams loud enough so that forms will need to be filled out, and the bear will be assassinated because it's become fond of campsites. Be kind to bears. I remember throwing plums out the window of Dave's Chevy at a big black bear when I was a boy. Thing came and put its paws up on the roof of the car and stuck its snout into get the rest of the plums, and maybe a bit of the boy. Terrifying.

Life is full of terrifying things. I poke the fire and fret, trying to stop nutting out about how *long, difficult and fast* this life is. There is a mid-life crisis that comes like a big wave to destroy homes and upset the whole damned family. We always want what we don't have, eh? I wonder if Bono wishes he were pot-bellied with an anonymous wife and kids and house in the suburbs. I wonder if he can find a campsite away from the hustle... Oh, I guess he probably has his own island.

Summer's over. Can my ageing colleagues and I manage to keep throwing blues dances for more than just divorcees and alcoholics, or will middle-age turn us all puffy and dull like Phil Collins? If a modern working bluesman is still onstage in his forties, he shouldn't just be playing to divorcees and alcoholics. He's gotta be good enough to entertain the greater stinking public. There'll be no time for the starving artist game as you get old. You have to pay for new teeth if you've been biting off bottle caps for 20 years. Some of these men and women even eat glass, or chew the heads off serpents.

In the forest by the sea, with the bear shit (called 'scat') and beer, the valley echoes with the roar of a biker's loud hog on the highway. Someone in the campground hoots and turns up the classic rock in the truck, then turns it down as it puts everyone gently to sleep. Polite loogans. I can just hear some Eric Clapton as I drift off. That should keep the bears away.

I snore in the pup tent and dream of a cruise ship somewhere where they play Desmond Dekker and Toots and The Maytals, sailing me up to an island in the sky...

Now rush back to Big Island (where dear reader likely sits on the toilet and reads this paper). Now the author is in a little cave on a horsehide on the pavement under a stage. A weird ska band plays over my head, fronted by an infamous gallant debaucher, and a company of freaks, whom thousands of people crowd the streets to party with every August Bank Holiday weekend. Drunk, sarcastic young women lurch in an out of the den and some appear to be on drugs. The leading lady maintains grace, while others roll on the concrete. Fifty-year-old men build and maintain a bizarre movie set around the stage and sound system. They climb on it and control it like stoned pirates and carry out the ritual. Broken glass, squashed tins and empty coconuts fill the gutter. Riot police and modern black soundsystems for two square miles in any direction. Gaz's Rockin' Blues on Talbot Road is swinging.

A big cigar has its effect, and my worries and thoughts rush in again. How long can the man up above keep making the girls dizzy and whipping up the crowds before he caves in to mid-life responsibility? It appears he's dodged it completely, the tricky bastard! Three generations are dancing to a Cuban ska-style 'A Message To You Rudy'. Genius. Natty Bo grins a gold tooth.

This pain in my knees won't heal. My back is killing me from carrying one of my many blues-children in a sedan chair above the crowd while she waves her machine gun and Sandinista flag. My eyesight is getting blurry. The raging crowd outside is freaking me out.

Should I try to find a nice lady and settle down? Who do I see around me, hmmm?

Angry English women singing "fuck you very muuuch" don't do it for me. They will have bitter frown-lines, troubles with alcohol, and will be forgotten and ignored soon, no matter how much money they spend on maintaining their image. I wonder if that lady is going to suffer a mid-life neurosis like this pathetic wretch in a hat. I wonder if her bladder will start failing soon. I wonder if she's going to have to get up to pee twice in the night or wet the bed. That happens to some women. Or they pee when they laugh, especially cynical laughter.

It's amusing when a new rock star arrives on this island with a ridiculous haircut, untrained shouty voice, catchy pop recipe, silly jeans and says, "I'm the toughest." (La Roux? Sounds like 'Upside Down' by Diana Ross.) It's a good tactic to come in with brass knuckles and bite somebody on the cock. But there's always an old guy with bloody trousers standing in the corner, who's been there for decades, because he's either got everyone working for him, or he's tough as beef jerky, or both. You won't get his cigarettes. He's in for life.

Alcatraz. But just the day before, I lay in Loogan Forest by the sea, dreaming of a paradise where grown men don't wear t-shirts and Nikes, and young women don't talk like old whores. Will I ever find paradise; a lush green island free of Yahoos and classic rock stations, free of military coups, and free of sloppy drunks?

The police come and shut down the Cuban Revolution party. Reminiscing and smoking are all we can do until the crowd thins. Then I wander home to bed and out of danger. It's a beautiful night with not too many fights to avoid on the way home. Wonder if anyone died at Carnival this year.

I sleep finally and, in the morning, a Mambo wakes me up like a noble hard-on. I'm off to make millions, and buy my own island big enough for bears, peacocks and my own damned campground full of hand-picked, well-aged but vibrant blues heroes. Read the sign: no bikers, no hippies, no riot cops, no religion, no bling, no photographers, no cats, no begging, no liars, no rednecks, no models, no track suits, no glow sticks... this will be my year. The kids can go hang themselves for fame. Long distance, baby, you gotta stay on your feet if you want to live with bears or humans.

WHAT IS THIS FIGURE IN BLACK WHICH
STANDS BEFORE ME, POINTING?

Issue 24, December 2009

Black Sabbath haunts this afternoon here in my blues hideout. As the rain and church bells of their self-titled 1970 album swell up, I fondly recall a gang of metalheads mugging me. My date was taken into the bushes and molested. Sabbath blared out of the ghetto blaster that I was beaten in the head with. We were young but strong enough not to let it give us a bad trip.

News from back in the Midwest colonies this week: two teenagers stabbed; bank robbed; pensioner beaten with table leg. Native and biker gangs are bigger than ever. London may be a tough place, but it's the same walking on the wrong street in Wintertown late on a Friday night. Reason and morals aren't there, and you will be curb-stomped to a gangsta soundtrack. Nothing changes except the soundtrack.

Which brings us to a question: How in sonic hell does a volunteer music journalist measure progress? Does music get better or just change? Is there any point to the change? Does it actually change much?

I know this is going somewhere, even if you don't. Who's your daddy? It's a good question — one that's recently been asked by the good folks at EMI.

I have a new job with EMI. I'm head of advertising. They've hired me on a reality ad I've just cooked up. We'll fake Paul McCartney's death again. We get him axed by a teenage gang in Kilburn who claim they didn't know who he was. Secretly, they're working for Pakistan Intelligence (who were in on the Twin Towers toppling). Then Paul gets found alive and well in a cave in Afghanistan. You see, we need something to compete with the Jackson ad (brilliant; an old ad-man mate of mine did that one), which has distracted everyone from buying the Beatles re-release. Poor EMI need a fresh angle.

Once upon a time, there was a fellow named Pasquali in Italy who discovered that if he brought noodles over from the Far East, people would eat them all up very quickly. He began to make noodles, and Italian food became Italian food. A thousand years later, Italian food is still the same.

Music, handbags, sunglasses and all sorts of crap are ruled by the same principles as Italian food. A good invention won't ever sound or look or taste bad. A good sound isn't relative to what decade you live in. It's good and that's that. Just like gnocchi gorgonzola will always taste good, if it's made properly.

On my 27th birthday, a long time ago, I took my stoned friends paintballing. We put on our urban nightmare costumes and giggled and went into the post-apocalypse-styled battle zone. I handed the nasty man who ran the place a CD of Arthur Lyman to play for us while we murdered each other.

"I only got a tape deck," he said.

"Oh, that's okay," I told him, "what tapes do you have?"

"We only got one tape."

"Uh huh, what's that?"

"Black Sabbath. First album."

Scary music is like Italian food. Turn it up, my friend, it's my birthday! Crikey, and an acid flashback. Hell couldn't be more fun than this.

Now keep your eye on the birdie. If tough guys change their tune, why doesn't Italy change its menu to sushi? The answer, not surprisingly, lies in the Vatican. There is a religious-right plot to keep us buying silly new handbags, metal, rap, and techno, while pizza and The Beatles are sold until the end of civilisation as part of the unchanging fabric of papal supremacy.

My advice to the kids is this:

1. Distrust everything expensive.

2. Love no one who isn't sceptical a good portion of the time.

3. The 1980s are not to be bought again, and you will be hurt if you

wear elf boots.

4. Don't work overtime to support the ageing establishment.

How will the new economy affect your mind? You can listen to whatever tunes you want, whenever you want, but it's not yours. You can drive where you want in a car bought on credit, and pay by the mile and zone. Everything — your phone, health insurance, home, entertainment and livelihood — belongs to the company, bank or state. So the solution is not to live in credit. The solution is to own simple tactile things and to use them to their full potential before throwing them out. The solution is to buy property as a group, avoid all hype and religion, and live off the waste of the wealthy.

But I'm miserable and haven't followed my own advice. The kids are stabbing each other more than ever before. We need population control. Music control. Stop the machine. Stop the press. Stop the bank. Stop grinning and laughing at me. I swear this McCartney ad will be my last. Then I'm out. One more drink and I'm going home and never coming here again. (They've heard it all before down here at The King's Head.)

Safe in my lair. Sabbath sounds soft now, nestled in the 1970s, and Ozzy never did any real damage. Gangsta rap is being laughed at as 50 Cent is making 'success at business' books. The soundtrack to our nightmares changes, but doesn't get better. It just changes, like this autumn's ugly handbag.

I've told EMI to put out some Beatles salad dressing. I have the albums still, but I need some salad dressing.

RING OUT THE OLD, RING IN THE NEW, RING, HAPPY BELLS, ACROSS THE SNOW

Issue 25, March 2010

Out with the old, in with the new indeed. My baby's buying more shoes she doesn't need.

We are now poised for victory, or at least a really good fight. I'm not one for calendar-changing parties, but for those who think of things in terms of new years and decades, you can rejoice. We've lived through so much garbage that we're finally due our reward. Yes, it's really time to buy that new/used accordion and simple country dress, go down to the river and to hell with the rent. This year is going to be the best ever!

What have we just been through? "The digital decade," I heard it called. Puke the bed if that wasn't the most hyped-up, hollowed-out shite that ever wasn't. The noughties tried soooo hard to be something new and improved. Every bluesman in the field was forced to take on twice as many gigs while the record business crashed and burned and only Pop Factor cleaned up.

In the last 10 years:

* Television comedians turned to bum tonguing and gang-rape jokes while the audience cringed and rented Marx Brothers movies.

* Black America became musically lo$t; celebrating pure materialism, unable to find a melody, losing all sense of purpose, and being completely duped by the man that makes the Benz.

* Alternative rock tried grotesque masks and zombie sex while the audience rediscovered fifties R&B and Cumbia.

* Brit Art crawled up its own pee-pee while filming itself for display in the Tate. The audience yawned and bought some watercolour paints and a pad of paper.

* The government spent £17b preparing for Mad Cow Disease,

SARS, Bird and Swine Flu, and culled 900,000 children arriving from Asian countries. The audience caught a cold.

* We were so bombarded by television talent shows that they can only become passé (although there are still a couple years left of aggressive dance competition; four dance troupes together on a phoney island where they must kill locusts by swinging the little urban kid in the air).

* We were so betrayed by capitalism, America, Conservative/ Labour governments and our business chiefs that evolution or civil war is now inevitable.

Yes, for once I am hopeful and happy. They completely saturated the market with exploding breast implants and people want their money back. I look forward to the coming years of riots, the popular rejection of what's called 'news', and the return of turntables in nightclubs. I can't wait for the bitching and moaning as MP3 players are replaced by streaming media on yer pPhone.

But these new gadgets will fail to impress. Watching telly on your handheld will come and then what... levitation? Short of that, nothing will be new. It thrills me to think that people might have nothing new to buy. With over 90 years of pop culture now at our fingertips, nobody can fool us into thinking that the Next Big Thing is anything more than a cynical hybrid of past styles with a salty lack of purpose.

I look forward to middle-class panic and identity crises as they find it harder and harder to distinguish themselves from the poor slob down the street. Anyone can have a Sony Gadget and shiny clothes made cheap in the third world, but only the super elite can wear the luxury brands. And those nitwits will be getting richer, giving us an increasingly clear target for our hatred (or lots of money to play at their awful parties).

In the coming years, the 'war on warming' will further become our daily burden. Save your tin cans to make heat deflectors! But, optimistically, the greatly exaggerated threat of religious fundies will settle a bit. This time, we won't let our politicians and oilmen invade Yemen or whichever new bogeyman training ground they invent. The public won't swallow any more phoney excuses for going to war until the climate gives us real reasons to invade... Spain. The struggle for fruit and vegetables will be real and the Spanish guerrillas will be holding our nation to ransom for ripe tomatoes in wintertime. The sultans of Dubai will pay much more for them than we can afford and we'll need to move in the fruit troops.

Everyone will hate the Israelis, but we'll all have a Jewish agent. The Catholics will campaign for popularity in Africa by endorsing matrimonial condoms handed out like wafer at the wedding. Holy population control. The Chinese will breed with the Africans to make a master race. The Shia and Sunni sects will have equestrian and camel Olympics in Dubai attended by the Royal Families from all good oil-purchasing nations. Our Queen will ride the winning camel.

Oh Lord, I think I like calendar-changing events now. All this predicting and reminiscing! This summer will be the BEST EVER! We are going to dance our asses off and turn the Bank of England into a giant flea market.

Minus 40 degrees outside on New Year's Eve. My East German Farm Girl and I had tried to leave the party twice. There were no taxis or buses and it was cold enough that the Prosecco under my arm would freeze in 10 minutes. We resigned ourselves to make the best of the situation by just playing cards down in the costume room. Five other people had the same idea. The DJ upstairs had six million MP3s in his phone but couldn't find one we wanted to dance to. Best to sit with a small table of strangers and drink and laugh.

She and I played blackjack. The women at the table drank and drank until they were comparing cleavage and knocking the beer over. The cards became wet and difficult to play with, or marked with cigarette burns. Our new friends howled and fought. More strangers joined and left, each leaving with a wet lap and lipstick on their teeth.

We had a world of costumes to try on but didn't bother. Too easy. We had all the loose women and booze we could ask for but we didn't bother. Too easy. We just played cards, stuck in there, happy that the weather outside kept us from an endless number of destinations we didn't have to choose from. It's that which limits us that makes life enjoyable, not endless possibility.

We eventually struggled back to the igloo and did very, very kind things to each other. We woke up with only mild hangovers and full of hope. This is going to be a good year with the worst all behind us. New Year's Eve is behind us. The worst party of the year passed without too much pain. The best is yet to come, as love will burst the heart of Old Man Profit and a bright young thing will replace Old Lady Lies.

Sometime this decade I look forward to being paid for writing in this alternative press publication. Maybe the advertising department will get Apple to put in an ad for its new streaming media player. I look forward to spending that little bit of cash on an overpriced Sam Butera 45rpm record. When you're smiling, the whole world smiles with you. But this crooked grin is mine, all mine!!!

ALSO AVAILABLE FROM
JUNKO PARTNERS PUBLISHING

GRACE UNDER PRESSURE
& Other Stool Pigeon Stories